THE MARSHALL CAVENDISH
☆ ☆ ☆ ILLUSTRATED ☆ ☆ ☆
ENCYCLOPEDIA OF
WORLD WAR II

VOLUME 20

THE MARSHALL CAVENDISH
☆ ☆ ☆ ILLUSTRATED ☆ ☆ ☆
ENCYCLOPEDIA OF
WORLD WAR II

Based on the original text by
Lieutenant Colonel Eddy Bauer

CONSULTANT EDITOR

Brigadier General James L. Collins, Jr., U.S.A.

CHIEF OF MILITARY HISTORY,
DEPARTMENT OF THE ARMY

MARSHALL CAVENDISH CORPORATION/NEW YORK

CONTENTS

Editorial Director: Brian Innes
Editor-in-chief; Brigadier Peter Young, D.S.O., M.C., M.A.
Managing Editor: Richard Humble
Editor: Christopher Chant
Art Editor: Jim Bridge

CHAPTER 161

The War in China

△ *On the Salween front in north Burma: men of Marshal Wei Li-huang's "Y" Force, an army group 72,000-men strong operating from Yunnan, move up supplies. Early in 1944 "Y" Force was authorised to advance south into Burma to link up with the Sino-American forces under Lieutenant-General Joseph Stilwell, finally freeing the vital Burma Road from Japanese control.*
Previous page: Generalissimo Chiang Kai-shek, head of the Chinese war effort against Japan since 1937.

Japan had been pursuing a policy of economic penetration and military intervention in China since 1931. Her victory in the Russo-Japanese War of 1904-5 had established her as a great power, and during the next quarter of a century, Japan had become a powerful military and industrial nation. China, however, was still an ancient empire, stagnant and decaying, and did not progress at anything like the same rate as Japan during this period, although in the late 1920's, most of China was united under the political and military leadership of Generalissimo Chiang Kai-shek, who initiated a programme of military, economic, and industrial reform. In December 1936, Chiang reached agreement with Mao Tse-tung to end the civil war with the Communists, and it was at this point that Japan decided to overthrow Chiang and capture

China. This was, in effect, the start of World War II. Japanese troops, ostensibly on night training manoeuvres, attacked unwary Chinese troops guarding the Marco Polo Bridge at Lukouchiao, near Peking (Peiping) on July 7, 1937. Fighting intensified as the Japanese Government refused the Chinese National Government's offer to negotiate, and sent more

troops to northern China. Japan refused to admit she was involved in a war, although her troops occupied Peking and Tientsin, saying they were merely re-establishing law and order in China.

The Chinese National Government's army numbered two million poorly trained and equipped troops. The Chinese Communist army, comprising 150,000 guerrilla troops in north-west China, at first supported Chiang against the Japanese, but they too lacked modern equipment. There were no trained reserves, no navy, and only a few obsolete aircraft with inexperienced Chinese and foreign mercenary pilots. Raw materials existed, but factories capable of turning these into weapons did not. China's great asset was

△ *Chinese troops move up towards the front in Yunnan in 1943.*

◁ ◁ *An American poster calls for help for China, the first nation to resist Japanese aggression.*

◁ *Three men of a Chinese air-transportable infantry unit inspect the device on an American airman's flying jacket. This notice told the reader that the wearer of the jacket was friendly, and was intended to safeguard American aircrew in the event of their being forced down in an area whose inhabitants were unfamiliar with Americans and did not know of the existence of the war. The aircraft to move Chinese air-transportable infantry came from the India-China Wing, Air Transport Command, U.S.A.A.F.*

▽ *The Americans supplied the Chinese Army with most of its equipment, and set up training establishments to teach the use of modern weapons. Here Brigadier-General Thomas S. Arms, head of such a school in Kwangsi Province, shows an American rifle to Chiang Kai-shek (in cape). At the left is General Pai Ch'eng-hsi, deputy chief-of-staff of the Chinese Army.*

▽ *Chiang Kai-shek and Lt.-Gen. Albert C. Wedemeyer. In autumn 1944, the Japanese launched a major offensive in East China, and when Roosevelt suggested that Stilwell be appointed head of all Allied forces in China in an effort to halt it, Chiang demanded Stilwell's recall. On October 18 he was replaced by Wedemeyer, then a major-general, as Chiang's chief-of-staff and head of the new China Theatre that replaced the China-Burma-India Theatre.*
▷ ▷ *Chinese troops watch a training exercise.*
▷ ▽ *Ceremony to mark the arrival of the first convoy over the Stilwell Road from Namkam to Kunming on February 4, 1945.*

her population of 500,000,000, but her agriculture could produce barely enough food for all these people.

Japan's army consisted of about 300,000 regular troops, equipped with modern weapons, and 150,000 Mongolian and Manchurian troops, commanded by Japanese officers. Japan had two million reserves, a powerful, modern navy, and efficient air arms. Her factories were capable of turning out considerable quantities of weapons and equipment although she was dependent on foreign sources for raw materials.

Japan was confident of victory. Troops were landed at Shanghai on August 8, 1937, but met determined Chinese resistance. Japanese reinforcements were

rushed to Shanghai, but even so, the Japanese were pinned to their beach-heads outside the city for several weeks, and Shanghai was not captured until November 8. The Japanese then advanced up the Yangtze river towards Nanking, the capital, which fell on December 13, and the invading troops ran amok for several days. Chiang, however, had moved his capital to Hankow in central China, and to the surprise of the rest of the world, the government did not collapse. More fighting followed, and eventually Chinese regular forces and guerrillas under General Li Tsung-jen defeated a Japanese force of 60,000 in the Battle of Taierchwang. This victory did much for Chinese morale. The Japanese, though, were even

▷ *A Chinese gun crew in action with an American-supplied M3 105-mm howitzer on the Burma front.*

▽ *105-mm howitzers and their Chinese Expeditionary Force crews at an American training centre in India during 1943.*

more determined and advanced westward from Kaifeng to seize the important railway junction of Chengchow, preparatory to an advance down the railway to Hankow. In desperation, the Chinese broke the Yellow river dikes, and the flooding river drowned many troops, and destroyed supplies, tanks, trucks, and guns. The advance was halted, and the Japanese shifted their line of advance further south, to capture Hankow on October 25, 1938. Determined Chinese resistance resulted in the bloodiest fighting of the war in China. Chiang's capital was moved again, to Chungking, and the Chinese implemented a scorched earth policy in front of the Japanese, who seized Canton late in 1938.

Because the war was far-flung, inconclusive, and expensive, the Japanese changed their strategy. In 1939 they launched more amphibious operations, hoping to capture China's remaining ports and cut off her foreign supplies, and so precipitate the downfall of Chiang and his government. Accordingly, most of the ports were taken, but China still had two supply routes via which she could obtain supplies. One was along the narrow-gauge railway from Haiphong in French Indo-China to Kunming, and the other was through British Burma and then along the narrow, twisting Burma Road to Kunming. The Japanese soon cut the railway, and on July 18, 1940, Britain acceded to Japanese demands that the Burma Road be closed. However, it was reopened in October, after the defeat of Germany in the Battle of Britain, and with the support of America, which wished to ship

Generalissimo Chiang Kai-shek was born in 1887 and led the Chinese opposition to the Japanese invaders throughout the war. When Japan invaded China in 1937, Chiang was head of the ruling Kuomintang Party, with his capital at Nanking. With the overrunning and destruction of the Shanghai and Nanking areas, Chiang retreated into the remote western reaches of China. He continued the war against Japan from his new capital, Chungking. Chiang was made Chairman of the National Defence Council in 1939 and Chief of State in 1943. The Chinese struggle against Japanese aggression had long been admired by the Americans, but it was not until after Pearl Harbor that the U.S. could send China more than volunteer aid. It was not until 1943, however, when it appeared as though China might collapse, that the United States started to supply the Chinese Army on a massive scale. But this aid soon started to dry up when the Americans realised that there was probably a better case for developing U.S. air power in China than the none too efficient Chinese Army. Moreover, as a result of Chiang's ever worsening relations with Stilwell, his chief-of-staff, Sino-American relations deteriorated rapidly. But the Americans still expected Chiang's China to be the fourth of the great powers after the war–until the Nationalists were ousted by the Communists in 1949.

△ Chinese troops training in India hear a speech from Chiang Kai-shek on December 21, 1943, in which they were told that on their arrival at the front they would come under the overall authority of Vice-Admiral Lord Louis Mountbatten, Supreme Allied Commander, South-East Asia.

◁ March-past.

Lend-Lease supplies to China. In late 1940, the Japanese expanded their partial occupation of Indo-China and seized air bases from which their bombers could reach the Chinese section of the Burma Road, and to protect this, the "Flying Tigers" came into being.

In 1937, the Chinese Government invited recently-retired U.S. Army Air Corps Captain Claire Chennault to become its aeronautics adviser. He accepted and was appointed Colonel in the Chinese Air Force. He spent the next three years training Chinese and foreign mercenary pilots in his concepts of aerial warfare, but found it difficult to achieve decisive results while the Japanese had air superiority and he obsolete aircraft. He built up a reliable early warning system during this time by distributing radio sets to patriotic peasants, so that details of Japanese planes taking off in China could be relayed to his own headquarters, enabling his planes to get off the ground before they could be attacked.

As the Chinese Air Force was not a force in being, Chennault suggested to Chiang the establishment of a special air group of trained American fighter pilots. He enlisted some 90 volunteers for this from America, in addition to 150 qualified mechanics and administrators to serve as ground support, and they were known as the American Volunteer Group (A.V.G.). Chennault taught his team all he knew of Japanese aircraft and methods of warfare. America supplied P-40 planes under Lend-Lease, and some of the pilots painted eyes and a row of teeth on the planes, making them look like flying tiger sharks, hence the name "Flying Tigers".

In December 1941, Chennault sent one of his three squadrons to Kunming to protect the terminus of the Burma Road from air attack. Another was stationed at Mingaladon airfield in Burma to reinforce the R.A.F. The third squadron, the reserve, was rotated regularly with the others after they became active. By February 12, 1942, the "Flying Tigers" had shot down almost 100 enemy planes for a loss of 15 of their own.

The A.V.G. was disbanded in July 1942, and was superseded by the China Air Task Force (with Chennault in command), which proved a worthy successor to the "Flying Tigers".

The Japanese suspended their operations in China during 1942, due to other offensives in south-east Asia. An occupation army of one million remained

in China to protect towns and railways. The Chinese, however, were in no position to take advantage of this inactivity, since they were desperately short of *matériel* and munitions. Guerrilla activity continued unabated, however, in Japanese occupied China and in eastern China, which was cut off but not overrun by the Japanese. At first, all the Chinese forces were united against the Japanese, but Mao Tse-tung's Communists seized the opportunity to increase their influence in areas occupied by the Japanese and thus out of contact with the National Government. In fact, guerrillas in north-western China had an unofficial truce with the Japanese, which allowed the latter to release troops from here and concentrate more forces against Chiang's army in central and southern China.

The weakness of isolated China was demonstrated by Japanese successes in minor offensives planned to give experience to new units, and also to take the Chinese rice crop. These "rice offensives" took place in unoccupied China and enabled the Japanese troops to obtain food easily, whilst depriving the Chinese.

◁ ◁ *Chinese poster: "The American airman, remover of the Japanese yoke".*
△ *Smiling faces: men of the 359th Brigade of the Communist 8th Route Army with captured Japanese 7.7-mm Model 92 (1932) heavy machine guns. Note that one of the soldiers has lost his right arm. When Japan invaded China, a truce was agreed in the civil war, and the Nationalists even went so far as to support the 8th Route Army under General Chu Teh. On September 25, 1937, in the Battle of P'inghsinkuan (in the Wutai mountains of northern Shansi) the Japanese 5th Division was defeated by General Nieh Jung-chen's 115th Division of the 8th Route Army. This was the only divisional-sized engagement fought by the Communists in the whole war.*
◁ *A Min Ping militiaman with a pair of home-made land mines.*

△ How Japan's Axis partner Italy saw the war in China: a painting from the June 7, 1942 edition of La Domenica del Corriere . . .

In December 1943, the Chinese managed to repulse a rice offensive in the Battle of Changteh.

China came within the area of American strategic and logistical responsibility. In 1942, Lieutenant-General Joseph Stilwell arrived in Chungking to head an American military mission to advise the Chinese Army. Chiang immediately made Stilwell his Chief-of-Staff, and sent him straight to Burma to command the 30,000 troops he had dispatched to help the British. The Chinese forces distinguished

themselves, but were forced to withdraw in the face of Japanese superiority. Stilwell learned of the Chinese will to resist.

In July 1942, the U.S. created the China-Burma-India Command, under Stilwell, for logistical and combat support to China.

With ground communications to China severed by Japan's conquest of Burma, the Americans arranged a long-range supply airlift from bases in north-eastern India to Kunming. Because of Japanese bases in northern Burma, the supply planes were forced to fly at 21,000 feet and

more over the eastern Himalayas. This route became known as the "Hump". At first, the airlift was quite inadequate for China's needs, as not many planes were available.

The supplies were needed by both Stilwell and Chennault. Chennault believed that victory could be obtained by air-power alone, and thought that he should have the bulk of the supplies, while Stilwell wanted to build up the army. He directed that supplies be shared proportionately, but Chiang disagreed and

supported Chennault. The result was that Chennault received the bulk of the "Hump" tonnage, which was increasing as more planes became available. Chennault was promoted and his command enlarged and redesignated the 14th Air Force in March 1943. Chennault was then able to gain air supremacy over most of China, and his bombers ranged as far as Formosa.

Early in 1944, 20th Bomber Command arrived in this theatre, comprising new B-29 "Superfortress" bombers, able to fly

△ *. . . and how the Japanese themselves saw it: infantry follow a Type 89B "CHIRO" medium tank over an improperly-demolished bridge.*

at 350 mph and to carry 20,000 pounds of bombs to targets over 1,500 miles from their bases. In June, they commenced the mission assigned to them at the Cairo Conference, namely to attack the home islands of Japan from bases in China. For this purpose, extra-long runways were constructed by Chinese coolies in Ch'eng-tu, and from here, 68 Superfortresses set off on their first raid on Japan on June 15 to hit a steel plant on the Japanese island of Kyushu. Owing to the difficulty of transporting supplies over the "Hump", the main bases of the B-29's were in India. Between raids on Japan, the B-29's attacked Japanese bases in south-east Asia from Calcutta. Commanding 20th Bomber Command was Major-General Curtis LeMay. He and Chennault worked together on joint operations and tried out a new bombing method with low-level incendiary attacks instead of high-level, high explosive bombing attacks.

Stilwell predicted that the Japanese would attempt to capture the air bases by ground attack, and to meet this threat,

the Chinese Army must be built up. Events were to prove him right. In the winter of 1943 and early spring 1944, the Japanese conducted a number of offensives. On May 27, 1944, the Japanese 11th Army, 250,000 strong, initiated a south-westward drive from Hankow to Ch'ang-sha. On the same day, the 23rd Army, 50,000 strong, struck west from the Canton area. This was the first large-scale offensive since 1938, and at first, Chinese resistance was stubborn, helped by the air attacks of Chennault's pilots. However, Ch'ang-sha fell on June 19. The Japanese met strong resistance at Heng-yang, which fell only after an 11-day siege, but after this, Chinese resistance disintegrated and seven of the U.S. Air Force's 12 bases fell into Japanese hands. The invaders then turned west towards Kunming and Chungking.

Stilwell desperately tried to reorganise the Chinese to resist more effectively, but there was little he could do about equipment as Chennault had claim to most of the supplies arriving via the route over the Hump.

Cross-country transport, Chinese fashion.
◁△ *A dismantled Lend-Lease jeep is portered over a mountain in Yunnan. Directing the operation is Captain Lui An (hands on hips), Chinese Foreign Affairs Bureau officer attached to the Chinese "Y" Force's American operations staff. After re-assembly, the jeep was used by Lieutenant-General Soong Hsi-lien, commander of the Chinese 11th Army Group, to reconnoitre roads to be used by captured Japanese transport.*
△ *Re-assembly starts.*
◁◁ *The rear wheels and axle of a six-wheel truck arrive in Kenanpo in Shansi Province.*

◁△ *General Wedemeyer addresses men of the U.S. 14th Air Force at their base at Hsi-an in Shensi.*

◁ *With a singular lack of heavy construction equipment in China some 300,000 Chinese men and women were drafted in to build airfields for the U.S. Air Force by hand. As soon as a runway was finished, the labourers moved on to build another, and U.S. aircraft started to operate against the Japanese. Seen here is a B-24 Liberator, a type that performed sterling work in this theatre.*

The inability of the Chinese to stop the Japanese alarmed Washington. Stilwell vainly recommended various measures to Chiang to reconstitute an effective defence. President Roosevelt urged Chiang to grant Stilwell full command of all armed forces in China. Chiang and Stilwell were bitter personal enemies, and Chiang answered Roosevelt's plea with the request that Stilwell be recalled to America and replaced by another American general. Stilwell was consequently relieved on October 18, 1944, and the China-Burma-India Command was dissolved. Major-General Albert Wedemeyer replaced Stilwell as commander of a new China Theatre, and as Chief-of-Staff to Chiang.

The Japanese drove on. In November, they captured Kuei-lin, Liu-chou, Nanning. The 14th Air Force was driven out of eastern China and forced back into the south, where the bases used by the B-29's were available, as 20th Bomber Command was transferred to the Marianas early in 1945.

In mid December, the Japanese advanced towards Kuei-yang, K'un-ming, and Chungking. Wedemeyer, however, got on with Chiang rather better than Stil-

△ *Chinese groundcrew at work on an American-supplied aircraft under the watchful eye of a sentry. Note the camouflaged dispersal huts.*

well had done, and persuaded Chiang to agree to the transfer of two veteran Chinese divisions from the Burma front, and these troops became the backbone of a revitalised defence. Forces were also brought from other parts of China, and in December, the strengthened Chinese ground forces, supported by the 14th Air Force, counter-attacked east of Kuei-yang, and this stabilised the situation. The immediate danger of complete defeat and the collapse of China was averted.

The strength of the opposition at Kuei-yang surprised the Japanese, and they called off their offensive to re-organise their forces and strengthen their lines of communication.

General Wedemeyer took advantage of the lull to reorganise the Chinese forces. He had an easier time than Stilwell, as the land supply route to China was now open again as a result of the successful Allied offensives in northern Burma.

January and February 1945 saw re-newed Japanese offensives in south-east China, when Japanese troops made wide gains in the coastal regions between Hankow and the French Indo-China border. Three more 14th Air Force bases were captured.

The railway line from Han-yang to Canton was also captured at this time. Chinese troops here were completely cut off from western China, and so had received very little new equipment, and were thus unable to stop the Japanese advance, despite repeated attacks by the 14th Air Force.

In late March, the Japanese attacked on a broad front between the Yellow and Yangtze rivers in order to capture the American air bases at Laohokow and An-k'ang. This move surprised the Allies, and the Japanese netted the rice crops and captured Laohokow town and airfield. Wedemeyer and Chiang rushed reinforce-

◁ *A Chinese-manned American M5 Stuart light tank on the Burma front.*
△ *American tactical training for the Chinese: Lieutenant William S. Levey of Birmingham, Alabama, lectures on grand tactics with the aid of Captain Shien Pei as interpreter.*

ments to the front. The Chinese counter-attacked and halted the Japanese drive in mid April.

The Japanese moved their offensive further south, towards the air base at Chihkiang, but were again checked by a Chinese counter-attack at Ch'ang-te on May 8, in which the 14th Air Force played a decisive rôle.

This was the first serious defeat for the Japanese in China for nearly two years, and, realising they were over-extended, the Japanese Government ordered the withdrawal of troops from south China. More Japanese troops were needed in Manchuria, menaced by the Soviet threat to enter the war.

Chinese counter-offensives during May cut a corridor to Indo-China, and by July 1, some 100,000 Japanese troops were marooned in the Canton area, a similar number having moved back into northern China. The air force continued to harass the Japanese until the end of the war.

The dispute over the distribution of supplies had strategic consequences beyond China. Concentration on the air force at the expense of the army meant the abandonment of the Burma invasion, and the loss of Chennault's air bases deprived Nimitz and MacArthur of expected aid in the Pacific.

STILWELL AND CHENNAULT.

△ *General Stilwell, holding an M1 carbine, in the front jeep somewhere in Burma.*
▷ *Major-General Claire Chennault displays the newly-designed "Flying Tiger" emblem of his 14th Air Force. The badge was designed by Sergeant Howard Arnagard, seen on Chennault's right, to commemorate the famous American Volunteer Group or Flying Tigers, who served with the Chinese before America's entry into the war.*

The personal relationships between Chiang Kai-shek, Lieutenant-General Joseph Stilwell, and Brigadier-General Claire Chennault played a major rôle in the shaping of events in the China-Burma-India theatre of war.

From 1937, Chennault was Chiang's aeronautics adviser. He became a colonel in and trained the Chinese Air Force, and he instigated the establishment of the volunteer group of American pilots who flew as the "Flying Tigers" in support of China against the Japanese. When America entered the war, this group was absorbed in the U.S.-China Air Task Force, Chennault rejoining the U.S. Air Force and taking command.

Stilwell arrived in China in 1942, to head an American military mission sent out to advise the Chinese Army. Chiang appointed him his Chief-of-Staff, and in July 1942, the U.S. created the China-Burma-India Theatre, of which Stilwell had command, to give logistical and combat support to China, and for control, under the British, of American and Chinese troops in India and Burma. Stilwell was therefore responsible simultaneously to the American Joint Chiefs-of-Staff, to Chiang, and to the British commander in India.

Stilwell went straight to Burma to take command of forces which Chiang Kai-shek had dispatched to help the British. During this time, Chennault and Stilwell met and worked together to plan the air support for ground forces in combat in Burma. The Chinese troops had to withdraw to India, and relations between Chennault

and Stilwell cooled as differences in their opinions over the way to win the war became apparent.

Japanese victory in Burma meant the closing of the Burma Road, and supplies could then only reach China by air over the Himalayas, and only in small quantities. Chennault believed his aircraft played a far more vital rôle than the army, and that Japan could be defeated by air power alone. He, therefore, must have the supplies. Stilwell could see the danger of the Japanese launching ground attacks to capture the airfields, and he thought the army must be equipped to meet this threat. He was also anxious to reopen the Burma Road so that more supplies could reach China, and wished to strengthen the Chinese land forces for an invasion of Burma

The Americans in China

General Joseph "Vinegar Joe" W. Stilwell was born in 1883. In World War I he had been an Intelligence officer, and after the end of the war specialised in Chinese affairs. He served 13 years in China between the wars, and when the U.S. entered the war, Stilwell was given command of the American forces in the China-Burma-India theatre to bolster the Chinese and British. In 1942 Stilwell was appointed Chiang Kai-shek's chief-of-staff. At first his major task was the safe-guarding of the Burma Road, the vital supply artery along which *matériel* was moved into China. But the Japanese proved too strong, and Stilwell's men were forced back into India, where the Chinese Expeditionary Force was trained and equipped by the U.S. in preparation for the counter-offensive. In 1944 the Japanese launched a major offensive in China, and when they overran the areas in which the U.S. 14th Air Force's bases were located, the Americans suggested to Chiang that Stilwell be made commander of all Chinese, as well as American, forces in China. Chiang refused vehemently and in October demanded Stilwell's recall. He was replaced by Major-General Albert C. Wedemeyer. Stilwell's final war-time post was as the commander of the U.S. 10th Army in the Pacific from June 1945. A hard man with whom to deal, Stilwell had made the best of a very difficult situation during the war in China.

△ *Chinese American groundcrew at work on a P-40 of the 76th Fighter Group at Kunming in November 1942. From left to right they are Staff Sergeants Pak On Lee of Portland, Oregon, George Lunn of New York, and Philip Pon of New York.*

Stilwell used his authority and directed that the supplies be divided proportionately.

Chiang entered the argument at this point. He agreed with Chennault, and thought that great dividends came from airpower. He also wanted to spare the army as much as possible, and disagreed with many of Stilwell's ideas on the reorganisation of the Chinese Army. The American Joint Chiefs, however, agreed with Stilwell, and directed that supplies be shared. Chiang was

not content with this decision, and Chinese diplomats brought pressure to bear on President Roosevelt, who sided with Chiang. As the result, Chennault had his way. He was promoted, and his command was enlarged and renamed the 14th Air Force on March 10, 1943.

Stilwell was very annoyed, but he obeyed the order, and henceforth, Chennault's fuel and ammunition requirements got priority over all other necessary supplies. Chennault was then

able to gain air supremacy over most of China.

Because of the diversion o supplies from the army to the air force, Chiang would not permit Chinese troops in China to participate in Stilwell's planned two-pronged offensive into north Burma, and only with reluctance did he countenance the advance of Chinese troops from India since this would not affect the supplies to China.

A further problem was the deteriorating relations between

WHAT THE 14TH AIR FORCE HAS DONE TO THE JAPS
4 JULY 42 TO 30 SEPT 44

— AIR COMBAT —

JAP LOSSES — OUR LOSSES

DESTROYED 1023 — PROBABLE 516 — DESTROYED 105

— OTHER JAP PLANE LOSSES —

TO GROUND FIRE 7 — DESTROYED ON GROUND 357

TOTAL JAP PLANE LOSSES — 1385 DESTROYED 625 PROBABLE

JAP CASUALTIES FROM June TO Sept 30th

24,479 TROOPS — 6122 HORSES

— JAP SHIPPING LOSSES —
SHIPS OF 100 FT OR MORE

DESTROYED 317 SHIPS 709,639 TONS — PROBABLE 103 SHIPS 200,350 TONS — DAMAGED 206 SHIPS 410,300 TONS

TOTALING MORE THAN 1,000,000 TONS!

SMALL SHIPPING LESS THAN 100 FT (NOT INCLUDED IN ABOVE)

DESTROYED 2260 SHIPS — PROBABLE 365 SHIPS — DAMAGED 2315 SHIPS

NAVAL VESSELS

DESTROYED 17 — PROBABLE 13 — DAMAGED 19

ECONOMY of SPECIAL OPERATIONS

2.5 lbs BOMBS SINKS 1 TON JAP SHIPPING — SINKS 1 TON JAP SHIPPING

The Nationalist Chinese and the Communists, which led Chiang to establish a blockade of Communist-held regions of China, thus diverting troops from fighting the Japanese. Chiang resented Stilwell's efforts to withdraw these troops, and he rejected Stilwell's suggestion that the Communists be incorporated into the Nationalist Army. Stilwell was dismayed by the incompetence and corruption which existed in the army.

Chiang and Stilwell therefore became bitter personal enemies.

Stilwell's prediction that the Japanese would attempt to capture the air bases in China was well founded, and Chinese resistence disintegrated in front of the advancing Japanese. All through the summer of 1944, Stilwell and his staff vainly recommended various measures to Chiang for an effective defence.

The American Government was very alarmed lest China collapse totally. Roosevelt saw now that Stilwell had been right in urging that supplies to China be shared between ground and air forces. He and the Joint Chiefs recommended to Chiang that Stilwell be placed in full command of all the armed forces in China. Chiang refused flatly, and demanded the recall of Stilwell to the United States and that another general be sent out in his place. Roosevelt had no option but to comply with Chiang's wishes, and on October 18, 1944, Stilwell was recalled. His place was taken by General Albert Wedemeyer.

△ △ *The 14th Air Force's early combat record.*
△ *P-40 fighters of the American Volunteer Group take off on a sortie against the Japanese.*

▷ *Key man in China's early struggle against Japan: Lt.-General Joseph W. Stilwell.*

Major-General Claire L. Chennault was born in 1898 and organised the American Volunteer Group (or "Flying Tigers") to serve with the Chinese before the United States entered the war. In July 1942, after America had entered the war, the American Volunteer Group was amalgamated into the rest of the U.S.A.A.F. forces now serving in China. By that time, however, they had succeeded in destroying 300 Japanese aircraft, thus slowing the Japanese advance. In 1943 Chennault was made a major-general and given command of the U.S. 14th (Volunteer) Army Air Force in China, and took part in the Washington Conference on Far Eastern strategy. By July 1943 Chennault's pilots had won air superiority in Eastern China, and thereafter supported the Chinese Army in its struggle to drive the Japanese back into the sea. In July 1945, however, after he had refused to disband the Sino-American wing of the Chinese air force, Chennault resigned his command of the 14th Air Force.

CHAPTER 162

The Burma Road: China's lifeline

Previous page: *A Chinese soldier supervises coolies as they repair a landslide on the Burma Road. Natural disasters like flooding and landslides made the journey more hazardous in the early years than the Japanese raids.*
▷ *Working with picks and shovels, labourers prepare to cut their way through a mountain. Manpower was one resource of which the Chinese seemed to have unlimited supply, and they used it to compensate for their lack of heavy road-building equipment.*
▽ *Not all caravans were motorised. Here porters with pack mules and balancing poles take a break in their journey.*

Throughout World War II, the vital problem of transporting supplies into China loomed large. In 1937-39, during the undeclared Sino-Japanese war, the occupation of the coasts of China by the Japanese stimulated intensive efforts to build supply routes from the interior of China to the outside world. Perhaps the most notable of these was the construction by the British and Chinese of the 681-mile road from the Lashio railhead to Muse on the China-Burma border, and on to Kunming. This highway, called the Burma Road, was made passable to motor transport in 1938 by the labours of thousands of Chinese coolies, and for three years, the Burma Road shuddered with the passage of several thousand trucks carrying war supplies to China.

Contemporary Burmese political leader however, regarded operations on th road with very little enthusiasm, t desire to keep the doors of Burma sh against foreign intruders being an o theme in Burmese history.

China was dependent on supplies fro abroad to enable her to continue in t war against Japan. As well as the Burn Road route, a trickle of supplies al reached China along the narrow-gau railway from Haiphong, in French Ind China, to Kunming. With the defeat France in Europe, though, Japan d manded and received from the Vicl Government the right to land forces French Indo-China. The Haiphong–Ku ming railway was closed in June 194

The Japanese followed this by deman

The American Piper L-4 Grasshopper observation and liaison aircraft

Engine: one Continental A-65 inline, 65-hp.
Armament: none.
Speed: 87 mph.
Climb: 450 feet per minute initially.
Ceiling: 11,500 feet.
Range: 220 miles.
Weight empty/loaded: 740/1,220 lbs.
Span: 35 feet 2½ inches.
Length: 22 feet 4½ inches.
Crew: 1-2.

ing the closure of the Burma Road, and on July 18, 1940, Britain, hard pressed by Germany, reluctantly complied. China was now virtually isolated, but Generalissimo Chiang Kai-shek and the Chinese people remained steadfast.

The Burma Road, fortunately, did not remain closed for long. Britain defeated Germany in the Battle of Britain, and Churchill, with the backing of the United States, which wished to ship Lend-Lease supplies to China, ordered the reopening of the Road on October 18, 1940. This was now the only supply route to China, and large quantities of American Lend-Lease military supplies began to arrive in Rangoon. From here, they travelled by steamer up the Irrawaddy, and by road and rail north through Mandalay to Lashio where they joined the Burma Road.

Air support from the "Flying Tigers"

Air-power is important in any theatre of war, but in Burma it was a dominating factor from the start. In planning at this time, great reliance was placed on the ability of air forces to halt, or at least to delay greatly, the advance of enemy columns. Over the next three years, however, this was shown to be a fallacy. Air attack alone could not stop the movement of either side. Even if it could, the Anglo-American air forces in Burma were not then of a size to attempt it. The air force in Burma consisted of only one R.A.F. squadron, equipped with Buffaloes, and a flight of the Indian Air Force having only a few obsolete machines. The Chinese Air Force also had a handful of antiquated planes. To redeem this situation, the American Volunteer Group (A.V.G.) was formed by Colonel Claire Chennault, Chiang Kai-shek's aeronautics adviser, its major task being to protect the Burma Road, which was extremely vulnerable to air attack. The A.V.G. base was in Kunming, China, but Chiang, realising the importance of Rangoon for the Burma Road, sent the 3rd Squadron of the A.V.G. to R.A.F. Mingaladon, near Rangoon. If the Japanese succeeded in occupying Burma and closing the Road, China's ability to resist Japan would be greatly diminished. The defence of Burma was thus impera-

△ *Winding up the contours of a Chinese mountain range: this aerial view of the Ledo or Stilwell Road illustrates the considerable geographical barriers that faced the Chinese and American engineers. The 478-mile road cost $148,910,000, and was officially opened in January 1945. In just under two years the United States Army would declare it "surplus property".*

△ Early days of the war in the Far East, and Rangoon docks are still full of Allied shipping. This was the first stage of the journey to China via the Burma Road.

◁◁ Lend-Lease goods wait in Rangoon. In the foreground are crated trucks for the road; in the background fighter aircraft are stacked in crates.

◁ An American ship in the Irrawaddy Docks in Rangoon. She still carries the Stars and Stripes markings which distinguished her as neutral before America's entry into the war.

tive. Without the flow of supplies over the Burma Road, the likelihood that the A.V.G. could continue to function effectively in China was nil.

The A.V.G. was equipped with 100 P-40 Tomahawk aircraft, supplied by America through Lend-Lease, and the airmen were hand-picked volunteers from the American air force. The pilots decorated their planes, which were consequently known as the "Flying Tigers".

The Allied air forces were contending against great odds, however. The Japanese aircraft were superior in number and range, but by February 12, 1942, the Flying Tigers had shot down almost 100 enemy planes for the loss of only 15 of their own, spurred on, no doubt, by a reward of 500 dollars for every Japanese plane downed.

On December 23, 1941, the Japanese launched their first raid on Rangoon. On January 20, 1942, after almost a month of bombing raids against Rangoon and other

military installations in Burma, Japanese land forces crossed the Thai border into southern Burma. Their purpose was to cut the link between Rangoon and Kunming and then to capture Burma. Rangoon was captured on March 6, 1942, and Lashio, the southern terminus of the Burma Road, fell on April 29, along with 44,000 tons of Lend-Lease supplies destined for China.

Japanese forces cut the Road

With the closing of the Burma Road, the only land routes to China were the old highway across the Sinkiang province from Russia, and the caravan trails across the Himalayas and through Tibet from India. Neither of these routes was ideal for transporting large quantities of goods to China. The route through Sin-

Life blood of the road, trucks (ready built or as engines and chassis) were quickly moved up to the Burma Road.
▽ A convoy of Chevrolet trucks leaves Rangoon.

◁ Local carpenters were conscripted to build the cab and body on these commercial chassis.

▽ Indian loaders at work at the Lashio dump. In the background are stacks of spring leaves, essential replacements for the broken springs which littered the road to Chungking.

kiang was over thousands of miles of over-loaded Russian railways, and although the caravan route through Tibet was a much shorter journey, only pack animals could traverse the mountain trails, which meant that heavy equipment could not be carried.

"The Hump"

The fall of Lashio was therefore a crushing blow to the Chinese, but they survived it through the establishment of the air lift over the "Hump" from India to China.

Pioneers over the Himalayan Hump to China from India were Colonels Old and Tate. After Colonel Old had made the first surveying flight, Colonel Tate proved it was usable by transporting 13,000 Chinese troops to General Stilwell in India during the 1942 monsoon season.

Operating between 16,000 and 22,000 feet with oxygen, the pilots flew through almost all weather, although sometimes monsoon rains and wind delayed the flights for days at a time. When the accident rate became high, Chinese pickets were paid so much for every pilot saved. Although the tonnage carried over the Hump was low in the beginning, the Americans stepped up the monthly average to 20,000 tons during 1943.

Even when the planes made their regular journeys, however, there were difficulties in moving the goods from Kunming to the forward bases of the China Air Task Force, which were situated in regions surrounded by Japanese, and defended only by poorly equipped Chinese armies. The China Air Task Force had superseded the A.V.G. in July 1942, and most of the Hump supplies were allotted to it as Chiang Kai-shek and Chennault believed that decisive results could be achieved through airpower alone.

For raids against Japanese installa-

▽ *Lashio railway station. Here the supplies were off-loaded from goods trains and on to trucks for the journey into China. The picture shows the three modes of transport available—human, animal, and motorised.*

tions in Burma, China, and Indo-China, the China Air Task Force needed a large amount of aviation gasoline. With the closing of the Burma Road, all fuel had to be flown in over the Hump, and then it had to be carried or rolled by Chinese coolies over hundreds of miles of dirt road to reach the air bases. To carry one day's supply of fuel from Kunming to Kuei-lin took 40 days if carried by cart, and 75 days if rolled by coolies.

On March 10, 1943, the China Air Task Force was enlarged and redesignated the 14th Air Force, still under the command of Chennault. Fuel was in very short supply at this time, not so much because of an insufficient number of planes to ferry goods to China, but due to bottle-necks along the route from Calcutta and Karachi to the airfields in Assam. Indian rail facilities were disorganised and inadequate to convey large quantities of goods quickly. There was also a delay on the part of the British to complete the necessary airfields in Assam on time.

The Hump airlift enabled the Chinese to

▽ *Indian labourers load bales of cotton on to trucks at Lashio. The road carried commerical as well as military traffic, for Japan controlled China's ports, and consequently the latter was forced to rely on the overland route for imports and exports.*

receive supplies to continue in the war. What had happened to the land forces in the meanwhile?

The land force commanders

In the last days of April 1942, the commanders (Slim, Stilwell, and Alexander) realised that they could no longer hold any line against the Japanese in Burma. The troops therefore withdrew to India, to do so undertaking a 20-day journey of hard foot-slogging through 140 miles of jungle and mountain.

On arriving in Delhi, Stilwell stated that he regarded Burma as a vitally important area for re-entry into China, and that it must be recaptured.

While the British and Chinese forces were struggling through the mountains into Assam, there were still six Chinese divisions in operation in eastern Burma, being vigorously pursued by the enemy. In the middle of May, it appeared that the Japanese were about to launch a major attack up the Burma Road, advance into Yunnan, and capture the terminus of the Road. They did not in fact do this, and later they denied they had any plans to do so, but Chiang and Chennault were convinced that a major attack was imminent. Before the end of April, Japanese units were pushing north from Lashio up the Burma Road with tanks and motorised infantry. Having swept aside Chinese opposition, they reached the gorge of the Salween river. Their advance was halted here, however, when the Chinese destroyed the bridge.

By the end of May the Japanese held

△ *Indian and Chinese drivers stop for a wash on the outskirts of Lashio. Their trucks would have been driven from Rangoon, and would be loaded at the dumps at Lashio in preparation for the 1,400-mile drive to Chungking.*
◁ *When the Burma Road was cut, aircraft began to fly supplies "over the Hump". Here an elephant demonstrates nature's answer to the fork-lift truck as it loads drums of fuel, vital for the U.S. aircraft operating in China.*

▽ *Trucks loaded with drums of fuel in the morning mist on the Burma Road. The journey was made without a break, except at night or at the customs barriers. The trucks would drive in convoy, though distances between each vehicle could be up to half a mile.*

Burma and were in a dominating strategic position. Though temporarily checked by monsoon rains, they were poised to attack either India or China, and could certainly bomb Calcutta, where most of the American and British supplies were concentrated.

Various plans were put forward at this time for the recapture of Burma. The American priority was supplies for China, by road or air, and they therefore wanted the offensive to take place in northern Burma. The Americans also favoured the construction of a new overland route to China, and planned a route for this. The British, too, had a projected road plan, but the American one was chosen, and the building of the road was assigned to the Americans. They possessed the necessary manpower, materials, and engineering experience on a large scale. Stilwell was made responsible for the road. The plans were drawn up by Brigadier-General Raymond Wheeler. American engineers, under the command of Colonel Arrowsmith and later General Pick, commenced work on the road on Christmas Day 1942, cutting the first trace at Milestone Zero, just outside Ledo. They aimed at reaching Shinbwiyang, 103 miles away at the head of the Hukawng valley, within a year.

The Ledo Road project was an ambitious scheme. It aimed at cutting a three-lane highway in gravel from Ledo, the rail-

Aircover and its vital concomitant, fuel.
◁ ◁ A Curtiss Hawk 81A-3 (P-40C) Tomahawk fighter is uncrated in Burma.
◁ Yunnanese coolies load drums of fuel at Lashio.
▽ Assembled fighters, less their characteristic "Flying Tiger" insignia, wait on an airfield in Burma. Capable of absorbing much battle damage, tractable but slow, the P-40 remains one of the controversial aircraft of the war.
Overleaf: Lashio stacked with Lend-Lease supplies. The depot was to fall on April 29, 1942 and with it some 44,000 tons of supplies were lost.

way terminus in north Assam, through the Patkai hills in north Burma, down the Hukawng valley to Myitkyina, across the Irrawaddy to Bhamo, where it would join up with the old British road from Bhamo to Namkham. It would then go on to the little village of Mong Yaw where it would meet the old Burma Road. The overall distance to the Chinese border was 478 miles. The eventual destination of the convoys, starting from Ledo, was Chungking, the Nationalist Chinese capital and Chiang Kai-shek's headquarters, nearly 2,000 miles away.

Building the road involved the most complicated engineering and extreme hazards. The uncharted track led through formidable country with cliffs, enormous peaks, hushed forests, and winding rivers. As well as geographical hazards, there were also extremes of temperature, and disease (including malaria, black-water fever, dysentery, and scrub typhus) was rife. Men fought disease by oiling, disinfecting, and spraying the countryside, but even so the sickness rate was high. Fits of depression were also common to the road builders. Yet progress was made in conditions that at any time other than war would have been intolerable. Life was not eased by the frequent infiltration of Japanese behind the Allied lines: balanced in high trees, they sniped at those working on the road, and seriously hampered progress.

American *matériel* paves the way

As the American engineering battalions—composed mostly of negroes with a cadre of white operatives—pushed forward, so the stream of men and *matériel* behind them increased. From America by ship to Karachi and Bombay, then across India by train, came more bulldozers, graders, sifters, caterpillars, medical units, supply units, and transport. From India and the hills, 50,000 coolies came to work on the road.

The monsoon season presented more problems. Rain fell at the rate of up to 15 inches per day, and this led to floods and landslides. Mules and vehicles got bogged down, and bulldozers were lost over collapsing steep banks. The men, wet all the time, slept in waterlogged tents or jungle-hammocks. The soggy

▷ *Trucks queue to be loaded for their journey to Chungking.*
▷ ▷ *A suspension bridge, complete with Nationalist Chinese symbol and blockhouse and guard. U.S. aircraft destroyed the bridge over the Salween gorge to delay the Japanese thrust in 1942.*

▽ *A wrecked truck. Operators would cannibalise wrecks and rebuild trucks. Despite this, it was estimated that it took 2,000 trucks a month to replace those worn out on the Burma Road.*
▽ ▷ *A Chinese town over the border. The war in China was a curious mixture of the modern with the mediaeval.*

jungle became infested with long, purple leeches.

During the monsoon months, though, there was little likelihood of interference from the Japanese north of the Hukawng valley, and the Chinese 38th Division left its Ledo base and was deployed in front of the engineering group as forward protection.

Top priority status allocated

At the "Trident" Conference in May, 1943, the Combined Chiefs-of-Staff urged the importance of operations in northern Burma, and directed that an offensive designed to facilitate the building of the road should begin before the end of the year.

The Ledo Road followed the course of the fighting in Burma through the Hukawng and Mogaung valleys, and on to Myitkyina, which had fallen to Stilwell's Chinese and American troops in the middle of 1944. The road then had to be carried on to Bhamo, from where the Japanese had withdrawn, and then on to Namkham.

The Stilwell Road opens to traffic

On January 31, 1945, a ceremony was held on the Burma-China border at Wan-t'ing chen. With great fanfare and rejoicing, a convoy, largely composed of American journalists out on a spree, and the Chinese 6th Route Army, left for Kunming. The Ledo Road was now officially open.

Chiang Kai-shek proposed that the combined Burma and Ledo roads be renamed the Stilwell Road in honour of the man who had worked so hard to break the land blockade of China.

The value of the Ledo Road was questioned by some who doubted if it would ever repay the expenditure in men and resources devoted to it. Sadly, in November 1946, the Ledo Road was declared "surplus property" by the United States Army after the altogether vital part it had played in keeping China in the war.

▽ *China, destination of the Burma Road. The gate-house to the ancient ramparts of Shakwan, with fortifications from another age. Despite the depredations of the civil strife which had continued since 1911, the Chinese had faced the Japanese longer than any other nation in the East. For the first two years of the war with the West, the Japanese still maintained that the Chinese were the toughest troops they had faced.*

The Allies in Burma

1. *General "Vinegar Joe" Stilwell with Lord Louis Mountbatten, Supreme Allied Commander, South-East Asia. Stilwell was a difficult subordinate, and at times could be very outspoken.*
2. *Mountbatten with Generalissimo Chiang Kai-shek, the Chinese political and military leader.*
3. *General Alexander, G.O.C. Burma in the early days of the Japanese offensive, with General Wavell, C.-in-C. India.*

Press publicity both during and since the war has obscured the fact that Britain had several allies in Burma, from many nations. They fought for her both as regular and as irregular forces with considerable success.

Their battlefield was a country scored from north to south by broad rivers and steep mountain ridges. Road and rail links to India were cut or restricted at regular intervals by the monsoon. The monsoon lasts about five months and brings some 200 inches of rain. Vehicles bog down, roads are washed away, and men live in a miasma of dripping leaves, leeches, and mud.

Malaria dominates the area. Men exhausted by the fighting fell easy victim to its fevers. Casualties from disease, which included dysentery, swamp fever, and disorders carried by worms, snails, flies, and lice were in an approximate ratio of 14 to one man killed in battle. Prophylactic measures later lowered this ratio somewhat.

Coupled with these natural hazards was an enemy who had a reputation of being master of the jungle, dedicated to con-quest, and with an attitude to death in battle which was alien to Western troops. Life on earth was a mere staging post to a better world, and death for his Emperor would ensure him a place in heaven among his ancestors.

In the war in Burma, Britain's allies included the Americans, with their wealth of equipment, expertise, and aircraft, and the Kachin tribesmen in north-east Burma, armed with 18th Century flintlocks.

The Kachins had remained loyal even in the grim days of the

1

Japanese invasion. They rallied to the old British frontier post at Fort Hertz, and here, under Colonel O'Neill Ford, who had spent many years in Burma, they built up a garrison of 700 with a perimeter of sub-units in local villages.

With their 16 British officers they raided, harassed, and deceived the enemy. When the Japanese sent out an expeditionary force to destroy them, a skilful deception plan led the Japanese to believe that a large British army based on the fort was moving south in force to attack them.

Later, stiffened with some Burma Rifles, they protected an emergency airstrip on the Hump route and then, under Stilwell's command, they covered the building of the Ledo Road.

The Burmese were divided between the few who worked actively for the Japanese, about five per cent of the population, and the majority who remained loyal but neutral, awaiting the outcome of the conflict. The Burma Rifles and Intelligence Corps, however, gave very valuable service for the Chindits and 14th Army. General Wingate said of the officers in the Burma Rifles that they "were the best set of officers, without exception, that he had met in any unit in the world".

However, for the first two years of the war the Japanese listed the Chinese as the best troops they had to fight. In descending order came the Australians, Americans, British, Gurkhas, and Indians.

In due time each nation learned to live and fight in the jungle, and the order changed very radically.

The Chinese had been at war with Japan for seven years, and regarded war in a way which at first seemed extraordinary to the other Allies. They believed in encirclement and subterfuge, rather than an assault which could be costly, for by their reckoning the war had lasted too long to be affected by some local operation.

Chinese troops under Stilwell operated in northern Burma. His was an unenviable task, for as Chiang Kai-shek's Chief-of-Staff and chief of Lend-Lease supplies to China, he was caught up in the politics of Chungking. His frustration boiled over in his papers where he wrote: "What corruption, intrigue, obstruction, delay, double crossing, hate, jealousy, skullduggery, we have

4

whom I would rather have ha
commanding the Chinese arm
that was to advance with min
Under Stilwell it *would* advance.

It was the Americans' ability t
get press coverage for thei
activities which did not hel
Allied relations. With the comin
of Mountbatten in 1943, Britis
readers began to hear more abou
the "Forgotten Army", but th
U.S. heard little of the 14th Army
American readers thought tha
the British were dragging thei
feet in Burma, waiting for th
Americans to recapture thei
colonial empire. Stilwell's earlie
well-publicised demands for a
offensive simply added to thi
impression.

Allied air co-operation, how
ever, was efficient and impressive
Air supply of ammunition an
supplies enabled the garrisons i
Kohima and Imphal to stay fight
ing though the Japanese had cu
their land communications, win
crushing victory, and then driv
forward towards Mandalay an
Meiktila.

The Air Commando of Colone
Cochran, U.S.A.A.F., gave logis
tic and ground attack suppor
to the Chindit columns deep i
occupied Burma. Mustangs
Mitchell medium bombers
Dakotas, 100 light planes, an
Waco gliders were used to put th

*4. Alexander, Wavell, and
General Slim in 1942. At that
time Slim was commander of
I Corps—later he would
command the 14th Army.
5. Wavell and Stilwell.
6. Stilwell takes lunch in the
field with Chinese staff officers
before the battle of Toungoo.
Note the tinned American
Lend-Lease rations,*
Inset: *Lieutenant-General Dan
I. Sultan, who superseded
Stilwell in China.*

had to wade through. What a
cesspool. What bigotry and
ignorance and black in-
gratitude."

Taciturn and crusty, tactless
and critical, Stilwell also gave
great assistance in the
reconquest of Burma. Without
his energy and leadership in the
field, the campaign in northern
Burma might well have proved
abortive.

Slim has said that "he had
strange ideas of loyalty to his
superiors whether they were
American, British, or Chinese,
and he fought too many people
who were not his enemies; but
I liked him. There was no one

5

7. *Stilwell with General Sun Li-jen on the Burma front. Though Stilwell could respect the individual fighting man, he loathed the politics of the Chinese high command, and their constant demands for more equipment.*

8. *Mountbatten with Major-General Orde Wingate, the originator and leader of the Chindit columns in Burma. Between them is an American liaison officer.*

men down in the jungle landing zones and provide flying artillery against Japanese troop movements and positions.

Indian soldiers fought with growing confidence during the Burma campaign. The Gurkhas and West Africans enhanced the reputations of their warrior nations. Well-led, they emerged as some of the hardiest and most loyal Imperial allies in that theatre. The shortage of British officers meant that by the end of the war many Indian and Gurkha platoons and companies were commanded by officers of indigenous origin. In a country and a climate which taxed the energy and willpower of European troops, the cheerful good humour of "Johnny Gurkha" was a constant and much needed tonic.

CHAPTER 163
Luzon

Despite the fact that Luzon, the "capita
island" of the Philippines, was the larges
Japanese-held island between New Guine
and Tokyo, the American planners had b
no means been unanimous in the opinio
that it should be recaptured. Admiral
King and Nimitz had argued that it woul
be better, once a foothold had bee
established in the Philippines with th
capture of Leyte and Mindanao, to by
pass Luzon and go straight for Formosa
General MacArthur was the passionat
champion of the liberation of all th
Philippine islands before making the nex
advance towards Japan. When it wa
decided to invade Leyte in October 1944
two months ahead of the original schedul
– MacArthur announced that he would b
ready to invade Luzon by the end c
December, giving the 20th as a provisiona
date. This was so much in advance of th
earliest possible date by which an inva
sion force could be deployed for a
assault on Formosa that it was decided–
fortnight before the troops went in o
Leyte–to invade Luzon.

MacArthur was forced to postpone th
date for the Luzon landing by the slov
progress of the battle for Leyte. Here th
American forces were bedevilled by sluic
ing autumnal rains, which converted th
island battlefield into a quagmire. By th
end of November the Luzon attack ha
been put back to the second week c
January: the 9th. In addition, it wa
decided to capture the island of Mindor
as a curtain-raiser to the main landing o
Luzon. This would mean that the Luzo
force would not have to rely on the floode
airfields on Leyte–apart from the flee
aircraft-carriers–to provide air cover fo
the landings. Mindoro, right on Luzon'
doorstep, would provide excellent "fron
line" airstrips for round-the-clock opera
tions; and its capture was entrusted to
specially-formed unit known as the West
ern Visayan Task Force. Consisting c
two reinforced regiments under the com
mand of Brigadier-General William C
Dunckel, it was to attack on December 1.
while the struggle for Leyte was stil
moving to its close.

During the three-day voyage from Leyt
to Mindoro the ships of the Task Forc
had to endure heavy *kamikaze* attacks
the flagship *Nashville* was badly damage
by a *kamikaze*, and Dunckel himself wa
wounded (though he was able to stay i
command). But the Mindoro landing wen
in according to plan on the morning of th
15th. It was unopposed; Dunckel's me

Previous page: *After the bombing and artillery barrage, the infantry moves in . . . Company E, 129th Regiment, 37th Division, advances into Tuguegarao, the provincial capital of Cagayan on Luzon island, June 26, 1945.*

The return to the Philippines in force . . .
◁ △ *Approaching the beach at Mindoro on December 18, 1944, an L.C.I. launches a barrage of rockets.*
◁ ◁ *On Luzon, U.S. Coast Guard landing craft unload troops heading for Manila. The beaches are already secured.*
△ *At Binmaley, on Luzon island, men and equipment continue to pour ashore as engineers struggle with a bulldozer (centre) in an effort to make the route inland easier to follow.*
◁ *An L.S.T. unloading heavy equipment at Blue Beach, Mindoro island, as American forces press home their attack.*

2719

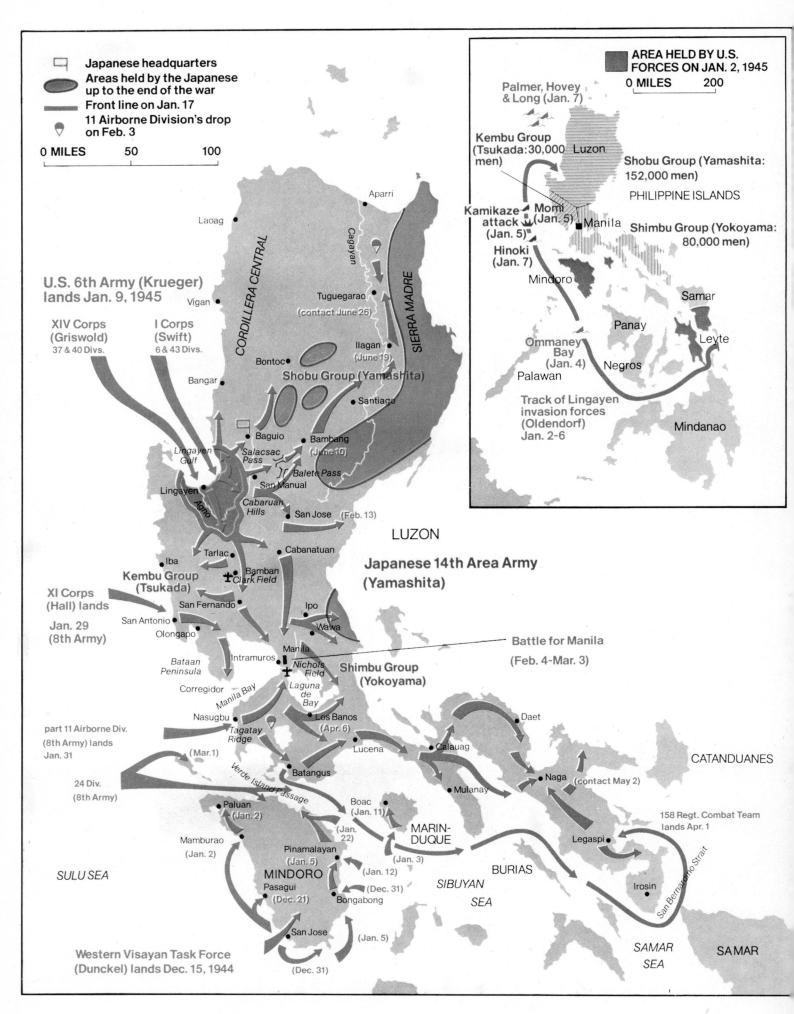

Japanese headquarters

Areas held by the Japanese up to the end of the war

Front line on Jan. 17

11 Airborne Division's drop on Feb. 3

0 MILES   50   100

AREA HELD BY U.S. FORCES ON JAN. 2, 1945

0 MILES   200

Palmer, Hovey & Long (Jan. 7)

Kembu Group (Tsukada: 30,000 men)

Luzon

Shobu Group (Yamashita: 152,000 men)

PHILIPPINE ISLANDS

Kamikaze attack (Jan. 5)

Momi (Jan. 5)

Manila

Shimbu Group (Yokoyama: 80,000 men)

Hinoki (Jan. 7)

Mindoro

Samar

Ommaney Bay (Jan. 4)

Panay

Palawan

Negros

Leyte

Track of Lingayen invasion forces (Oldendorf) Jan. 2–6

Mindanao

Aparri

Laoag

Cagayan

SIERRA MADRE

CORDILLERA CENTRAL

U.S. 6th Army (Krueger) lands Jan. 9, 1945

Vigan

Tuguegarao (contact June 26)

XIV Corps (Griswold) 37 & 40 Divs.

I Corps (Swift) 6 & 43 Divs.

Bontoc

Ilagan (June 19)

Shobu Group (Yamashita)

Santiago

Bangar

Baguio

Bambang (June 10)

Lingayen Gulf

Salacsac Pass

Balete Pass

Lingayen

San Manuel

Agno

Cabaruan Hills

San Jose (Feb. 13)

Iba

Tarlac

Cabanatuan

LUZON

Kembu Group (Tsukada)

Bamban   Clark Field

XI Corps (Hall) lands

San Fernando

Ipo

Japanese 14th Area Army (Yamashita)

Jan. 29 (8th Army)

San Antonio

Wawa

Olongapo

Battle for Manila (Feb. 4–Mar. 3)

Bataan Peninsula

Intramuros

Manila

Nichols Field

Shimbu Group (Yokoyama)

Corregidor

Laguna de Bay

Manila Bay

Nasugbu

Los Banos (Apr. 6)

Daet

part 11 Airborne Div. (8th Army) lands Jan. 31

Tagatay Ridge

(Mar. 1)

Calauag

CATANDUANES

24 Div. (8th Army)

Verde Island Passage

Batangus

Lucena

Naga (contact May 2)

Mulanay

Paluan (Jan. 2)

Boac (Jan. 11)

MARIN-DUQUE

158 Regt. Combat Team lands Apr. 1

(Jan. 22)

Mamburao (Jan. 2)

Pinamalayan (Jan. 5)

(Jan. 3)

Legaspi

SULU SEA

MINDORO

(Jan. 12)

BURIAS

SIBUYAN

Irosin

Pasagui (Dec. 21)

(Dec. 31)

Bongabong

SEA

San Bernardino Strait

San Jose

(Jan. 5)

SAMAR

SEA

SAMAR

Western Visayan Task Force (Dunckel) lands Dec. 15, 1944

(Dec. 31)

pegged out a large beach-head with no difficulty and work on the airstrips began at once, while the interior was still being mopped up. By December 23 two new airstrips were already in use on Mindoro and the build-up of aircraft for the Luzon attack could begin. To use MacArthur's own words, "Mindoro was the gate": the turn of Luzon had come.

Yamashita's problems

On paper, the Japanese force which would defend Luzon looked a formidable one: over 250,000 men of the 14th Area Army, commanded by General Tomoyuki Yamashita. But in fact Yamashita's prospects were not bright, and he knew it very well. Most of his units were under-strength and short of supplies. The virtual elimination of the Japanese Combined Fleet at Leyte Gulf meant that he would be getting no more supplies by sea. And the air battles during the prolonged fight for Leyte had whittled down the number of operational aircraft on Luzon to around 150. These would have no chance of halting the

American invasion force as it approached Luzon, let alone of commanding the skies over the land battlefield. Yamashita knew that his troops would not be able to stop the invaders getting ashore, and that he did not have sufficient men to defend the whole of Luzon.

In total contrast was the strength of the American forces. They were organised in the fashion which had launched the attack on Leyte. The land fighting was entrusted to General Walter Krueger's 6th Army – over 200,000 men, exclusive of reinforcements – which would be conveyed to its destination and shielded on landing by Vice-Admiral Thomas C. Kinkaid's 7th Fleet. The 7th Fleet – over 850 vessels strong – included the battle fleet, under Vice-Admiral Jessie B. Oldendorf, which had smashed Nishimura's battle squadron in the Surigao Strait during the battle of Leyte Gulf, and which was now to spearhead the invasion of Luzon by bombarding the landing beaches. Admiral William F. Halsey's 3rd Fleet would provide strategic air cover by launching carrier strikes on northern Luzon and Formosa, and land-based air cover would be the contribution of General George F.

◁ *American operations to clear Luzon.*

△ *A column of American amphibian tanks pauses along a road on Luzon. Despite the glum expression on the face of the Filipino at left, the original war-time caption enthuses " . . . natives greet the tanks and assure them that although their village was destroyed, they would much rather have the Americans than the plundering Japs".*

Kenney's Far East Air Forces, which would begin the battle from their bases on Leyte and Mindoro.

Bombardment and assault

It was obvious to both sides where the invasion must be directed: across the superb beaches of Lingayen Gulf, which was where the Japanese had landed their main forces in December 1941. Lingayen Gulf leads directly into the central plain of Luzon, to Manila and the magnificent anchorage of Manila Bay.

Yamashita was not going to attempt to meet the invaders on the beaches, nor offer them a set-piece battle once ashore. He grouped his forces in three major concentrations which, he hoped, would confine the Americans to the central plain. Yamashita's strategy, in short, was very like Rommel's attempts to "rope off" the Allies in the Normandy *bocage* after D-Day. But—as events in Normandy had already proved conclusively—the most

dogged defence was not likely to hold out for long against an invader with control of the air and uninterrupted supplies and reinforcements from the sea.

On January 2, 1945, the first ships of Oldendorf's bombardment force headed out of Leyte Gulf, their destination Lingayen. A punishing ordeal lay ahead of them, for they became the prime targets for Luzon-based *kamikaze* attacks which began on the 4th, while Oldendorf's force was still threading its way through the Sulu Sea. On that day a twin-engined *kamikaze* crashed into the escort carrier *Ommaney Bay*, damaging her so badly that she was beyond salvation and had to be sunk. On the 5th the American force was well within reach of the Japanese airfields on Luzon—under 150 miles—and the *kamikaze* attacks rose in pitch. In the afternoon, while the Americans were passing the mouth of Manila Bay, 16 *kamikazes* broke through the American air screen and attacked, inflicting damage on nearly a dozen American and Australian ships, including two escort carriers, two heavy cruisers, and two destroyers. Nor were

the Japanese attacks confined to aircraft alone; two Japanese destroyers appeared, but were seen off in short order. Air strikes from the escort carriers sank one, *Momi,* and damaged the other.

On January 6 Oldendorf's ships entered Lingayen Gulf and began to move into position for the bombardment—and the *kamikaze* attacks reached their climax. The weather was working for the Japanese. A low, dense overcast blanketed the airfields on northern Luzon, preventing Halsey's pilots from masking them with continuous patrols. Bad weather meant nothing to the Japanese pilots—except that their chances of immolating themselves on their targets were enhanced. By nightfall on the 7th two American battleships—*New Mexico* and *California*—three cruisers, three destroyers, and several other vessels had been more or less badly damaged, and three of them, fast minesweepers (*Palmer, Long,* and *Hovey*), sunk. But this was the last great effort of the *kamikazes* of Luzon. On the 7th, Halsey's planes battered the Luzon airfields so heavily that the last opera-

tional Japanese aircraft were withdrawn from the Philippines.

Oldendorf's ships had played an invaluable rôle in soaking up the punishment which might otherwise have savaged the troop transports and landing-craft bringing the invasion force. Now they went ahead with their bombardment programme, which raged for the next three days. Early on the morning of January 9 the troop convoys moved into Lingayen Gulf. At 0700 hours the final stage of the pre-landing barrage was opened and at 0900 the first wave of landing-craft headed in to the beaches. Shortly after 0930 the spearhead troops were ashore—but there were no Japanese troops to meet them. Yamashita had pulled back all his forces not only from the beaches but from the immediate hinterland, with the result that by nightfall on the 9th Krueger's army had established for itself a beach-head 17 miles wide, which reached four miles inland at its deepest extremities. And, true to form, MacArthur himself had landed in triumph, duly captured for

▽ *The build-up of equipment on Luzon continues—bulldozers and cranes roll ashore over a pontoon quay. Clearing obstacles from the main routes across the island and rubble from city streets was as important a task for these back-up forces as repairing and extending runways for aircraft.*

As they advanced inland, the
G.I.s came up against two factors
with which they were now
familiar: difficult terrain and
stubborn, costly, defensive action
by the Japanese.
△ Troops thread their way
through deserted rice fields near
Lingayen Gulf, Luzon.
▷ Infantrymen shelter behind
Sherman tanks as they advance
towards Japanese gun positions.

The American Curtiss C-46 Commando transport aircraft

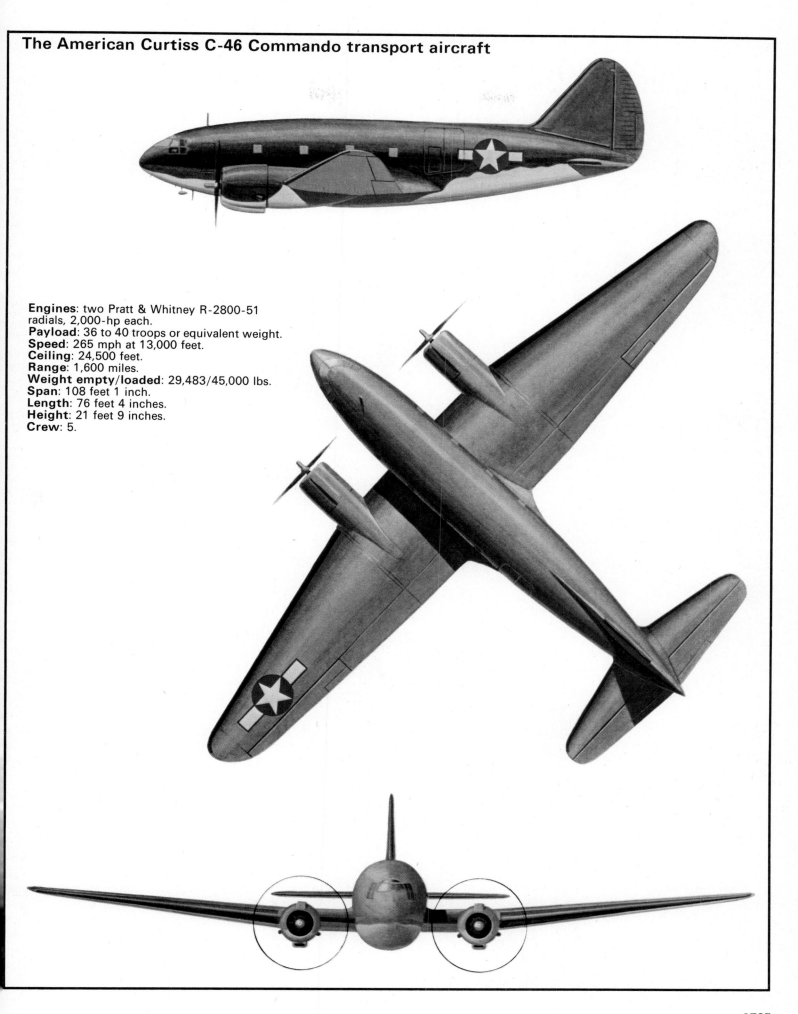

Engines: two Pratt & Whitney R-2800-51 radials, 2,000-hp each.
Payload: 36 to 40 troops or equivalent weight.
Speed: 265 mph at 13,000 feet.
Ceiling: 24,500 feet.
Range: 1,600 miles.
Weight empty/loaded: 29,483/45,000 lbs.
Span: 108 feet 1 inch.
Length: 76 feet 4 inches.
Height: 21 feet 9 inches.
Crew: 5.

posterity by the camera.

The 6th Army punch was a two-corps affair. On the right flank was Major-General Oscar W. Griswold with XIV Corps, consisting of the 37th and 40th Infantry Divisions. Griswold's corps had the task of breaking through to Manila and liberating the capital, a task obviously dear to MacArthur's heart. But before this could be done the left flank of the lodgment area had to be made secure from any heavy counter-attacks from the north, and this was the job of Major-General Innis P. Swift's I Corps (the 6th and 43rd Infantry Divisions). Until Swift had made the left flank secure, Krueger was going to take his time about pushing on to Manila—and he was wise to do so. For Swift's corps was faced by the "*Shobu*" Group, the largest of Yamashita's three concentrations, 152,000-men strong and well dug in along a chain of strongpoints 25 miles long, from Lingayen Gulf to the Cabaruan Hills. Foul weather on the 10th, ramming home the vulnerability of the landing beaches by causing considerable disruption, made it clear that Swift's task was of vital importance. But his progress against the tough Japanese defences remained slow, much to MacArthur's chagrin. Not until the end of the month did I Corps, reinforced with the 25th and 32nd Divisions, push the Japanese back into the mountains after a tank battle at San Manuel on the 28th. They reached the approaches to Yamashita's H.Q. at Baguio and drove east through San Jose to reach the eastern shore of Luzon, pushing a corridor across the island. This now cut off Yamashita from his troops in the island's centre and south.

Griswold and XIV Corps met with scanty opposition as they began their advance to the south. By the 16th they were across the Agno river, still with little or no opposition—but Krueger was yet unwilling to push too far ahead in the south until he was convinced that the northern flank was secure. But on January 17 MacArthur intervened, stressing the need for an immediate drive on Manila. There were plenty of good reasons. The Americans needed the port; they needed the airfield complex at Clark Field for Kenney's planes; and they were anxious to liberate the inmates of military and civilian prison camps before the Japanese had time to harm them further. But now Griswold's corps in its turn came up against the second of Yamashita's defensive concentrations.

◁△ *Troops from Blue Beach,
Lingayen Gulf, fan out into the
interior of Luzon island. Early
resistance was light, thanks to
the massive bombardment
mounted by sea and air.*
◁◁ *The still-smouldering bodies
of Japanese soldiers killed by a
flame-thrower. They were among
23 flushed out of their foxhole
by men of the 25th Infantry
Division.*
△ *Caught in a ravine, these
eight Japanese were picked off
by U.S. infantrymen using
small-arms. Three of the
Americans look down at the
dead enemy.*
◁ *Evidence of Japanese
atrocities in the Philippines—
the unearthed remains of some
3-400 Filipino men and women.
With their hands tied behind
their backs, the victims were
bayoneted.*

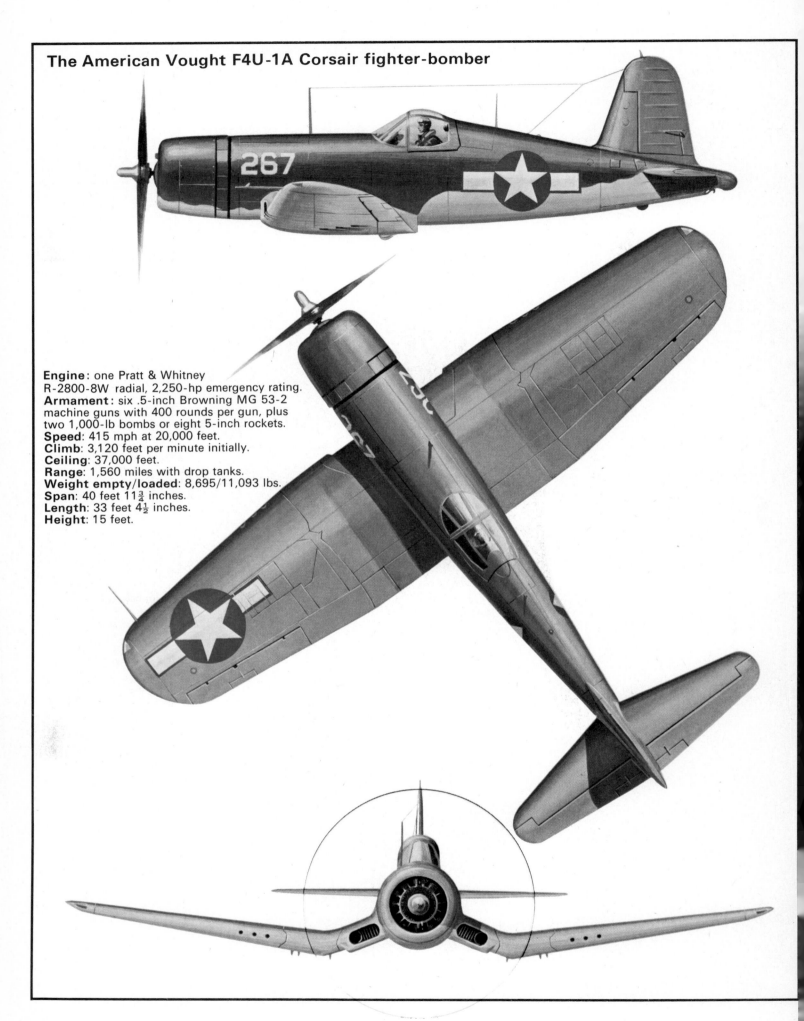

The American Vought F4U-1A Corsair fighter-bomber

Engine: one Pratt & Whitney
R-2800-8W radial, 2,250-hp emergency rating.
Armament: six .5-inch Browning MG 53-2
machine guns with 400 rounds per gun, plus
two 1,000-lb bombs or eight 5-inch rockets.
Speed: 415 mph at 20,000 feet.
Climb: 3,120 feet per minute initially.
Ceiling: 37,000 feet.
Range: 1,560 miles with drop tanks.
Weight empty/loaded: 8,695/11,093 lbs.
Span: 40 feet 11¾ inches.
Length: 33 feet 4½ inches.
Height: 15 feet.

This was the "*Kembu*" Group, 30,000 men under Major-General Rikichi Tsukada, stationed in the mountains west of the central plain of Luzon to defend the Clark Field sector. Griswold's corps first encountered heavy opposition from the "*Kembu*" Group at the town of Bamban on January 23. It took over a week of extremely heavy fighting before XIV Corps forced the Japanese back from Clark Field. By January 31 the "*Kembu*" Group had lost over 2,500 men and had been forced to retreat into the mountains; the Clark Field complex was in American hands and Griswold was able to resume his drive on Manila.

In the last days of January, two more American units landed on Luzon. The first was XI Corps, commanded by Major-General Charles P. Hall, consisting of the 38th Infantry Division and a regiment of the 24th Division. It landed on the west coast of the island to the north of the Bataan Peninsula, and its mission was to capture the Olongapo naval base and drive across the root of the Bataan Peninsula to Manila Bay. Unlike MacArthur in 1942, Yamashita refused to run the risk of getting any of his troops trapped on Bataan, but Hall's corps had two weeks of tough fighting before it reached Manila Bay. The second landing went in south of the bay at Nasugbu, 50 miles south-west of Manila. It was made by the bulk of the 11th Airborne Division; the plan was to tie down Japanese troops in southern Luzon and open up a second approach route to the capital. On February 3 the rest of the division dropped inland, on Tagaytay Ridge; the division concentrated and moved north-east towards Manila, but was fought to a standstill as it approached the outskirts.

It was clear that if Manila was to be taken it would have to be from the north.

Battle for Manila

Once again the impetus came from MacArthur. "Go to Manila!" he urged on January 30. "Go around the Nips, bounce off the Nips, but go to Manila!" His exhortations went right down the line of Griswold's corps to the two divisions which would do the job: the 37th Infantry and the newly-arrived 1st Cavalry.

Their main concern and objective was the big civilian internment camp at Santo Tomas, which was liberated on February 3 by a "flying column" of tanks from the 1st Cavalry. The prisoners in Santo Tomas were in an unenviable position, hearing the sounds of a tough battle outside the walls and fearing the worst until an unmistakable American bellow of "Where the hell's the front gate?" was followed by 1st Cavalry tanks smashing through the entrance. Hard on the heels of 1st Cavalry came the 37th Infantry, which pushed through to Old Bilibid Prison and liberated 1,300 civilian internees and P.O.W.s. The northern suburbs of Manila were in American hands. But the battle for the city was only beginning.

In 1942 MacArthur had declared Manila an open city rather than turn it into a battlefield, and Yamashita had no intention of fighting for the city in 1945. But there were 17,000 fighting men in Manila over whom he had no control— they were not Army troops. They were naval forces under the command of Rear-Admiral Sanji Iwabuchi, who was determined to hold Manila to the last. He split his men into separate battle groups, gave each of them a section of the city to defend, and prepared for an all-out battle. A unique episode was about to be added to the history of the Pacific war: its only

◁ *The flamboyant General MacArthur took every opportunity to visit the troops in the front line and boost their morale. Here troops aboard the* Nashville *crowd the decks as he embarks in a landing craft to visit his men ashore.*

urban battle.

The Americans took some time to realise what lay before them, but a week of vicious fighting and rapidly-mounting casualties forced them to accept that there could be no question of taking Manila without cracking the Japanese out of their positions at the expense of the city's buildings. By the 12th, XIV Corps had forced the Japanese in front of them back into Intramuros, the old walled inner city of Manila. South of the city the paratroopers of the 11th Airborne Division had run up against tough defensive positions built by the Japanese sailors on Nichols Field. Here, too, an inch-by-inch struggle developed, with the paratroopers getting artillery support from the guns of XIV Corps to the north. It was an unrelieved killing-match, eliciting a grim signal from one of 11th Airborne's company commanders: "Tell Halsey to stop looking for the Jap Fleet; it's dying on Nichols Field."

Even after the 11th Airborne joined hands with 1st Cavalry on February 12,

the battle for Manila was far from over. Iwabuchi's sailors held on grimly both in Intramuros and the rest of the city and over a fortnight of murderous fighting lay ahead. It was given a fresh element of horror by the fact that the Japanese refused to evacuate non-combatants, and it went on until the very last flickers of Japanese resistance were stamped out on March 3. MacArthur's obsession with the recapture of Manila had exacted a terrible price. The Filipino capital lay in ruins. Civilian casualties have been set as high as 100,000. American losses topped 1,000 killed and 5,500 wounded. As for the Japanese defenders of Manila, they had upheld the fighting traditions of the Imperial Japanese Navy by dying virtually to a man.

While the slaughter in Manila was still running its course, the clearing of the island forts in Manila Bay had begun. First came the overrunning of the Bataan Peninsula by XI Corps, begun on the 14th and aided by a landing at Mariveles, at

the tip of the peninsula, on the following day. It only took a week to flush the scanty Japanese forces out of their positions on Bataan; compared with the carnage in Manila it was an easy task.

Corregidor, the strongest fortress in Manila Bay, was a different story. In May 1942 the American garrison had capitulated within 48 hours of the first Japanese landings on the island. In 1945 it took over ten days of bitter fighting before the Americans got the island back. Their assault went in on February 16, a combined parachute drop and amphibious landing which rapidly gained control of the surface defences. But the Japanese still had to be flushed from their positions underground, and the island was not declared secure until the 28th. MacArthur himself visited Corregidor on March 2. Ready as always with a memorable *bon mot*, he announced: "I see that the old flagpole still stands. Have your troops hoist the colours to its peak and let no enemy ever haul them down."

The three smaller forts in the Bay remained. On Caballo and El Fraile, horrible measures were taken to break the resistance of the Japanese when they refused to surrender. Diesel oil was pumped into their positions and ignited with phosphorus shells and fused T.N.T. Caballo was cleared on April 13, El Fraile on the 18th. The Japanese evacuated the third island, Canabao, and the Americans encountered no resistance when they landed there on April 16.

Three months after the first American landings in Lingayen Gulf the Japanese had been forced out of central Luzon, the capital had been liberated, and Manila Bay was clear to Allied shipping. But still the battle for Luzon was far from over. Yamashita still had 172,000 Japanese troops under arms. They held the north and south-east of the island; Manila itself was still within range of Japanese guns, and the dams and reservoirs containing the bulk of the capital's water supplies were still in Japanese hands.

Pilots of the 201st Mexican Fighter Squadron line up in front of their P-47's on Clark Field, Luzon, in July 1945.

△ The only street fighting of the Pacific war took place in Manila, capital of the Philippines. G.I.s pass through still smoking ruins in the city's suburbs.
▷ MacArthur and members of his staff stand amidst the ruins of the American hospital at Fort Stotensburg, Clark Field, after the Japanese had been driven back from the area.

Moreover, the Japanese still controlled the most direct sea route through the central Philippines, forcing any Allied shipping heading west for Manila to take an expensive 500-mile detour. Until these problems had been solved and Yamashita's forces had been ground down to total impotence, there could be no question of taking the next step towards Tokyo. The last stage of the battle for Luzon began.

The most urgent problem facing the 6th Army was the big Japanese concentration east of Manila. This was the *"Shimbu"* Group, under the command of Lieutenant-General Shizuo Yokoyama: 80,000-odd troops, based on the 8th and 105th Divisions. The bulk of the *"Shimbu"* Group, 30,000 strong, was dug in along the southern end of the Sierra Madre range along the line Ipo Dam–Wawa Dam–Antipolo, extending south to the great lake of Laguna de Bay. Griswold and XIV Corps launched the first determined narrow-front attack against this strong position on March 8, following two days of intense softening-up by Kenney's bombers. By the 12th, the 1st Cavalry Division had battered its way through the maze of fiercely-defended Japanese cave defences and was

relieved on the 13th by the 43rd Division, which kept up the pressure and, in conjunction with 6th Division, punched deep into the centre of the *"Shimbu"* Group's line. On the 14th, General Hall's XI Corps relieved Griswold on this front and continued the offensive. By the end of March, the 43rd Division had struggled through to the east side of Laguna de Bay and had completely unhinged Yokoyama's left.

Further to the north, however, the 6th Division failed in its drive to capture Wawa and Ipo Dams. It took the whole of April, in the face of indomitable Japanese resistance, for the 6th Division to struggle forward into position for a final assault. By this time the successes in the south enabled the 43rd Division to be switched north to add more weight to the next attack.

This was heralded by three days of saturation bombing which dumped 250,000 gallons of napalm on the Japanese positions. The attack proper was launched on the night of May 6 by the 43rd Division. In this battle the American forces were aided to the north by 3,000 Filipino guerrillas, who kept Yokoyama's left flank fully engaged. At last, on May 17, joint Ameri-

2733

can and Filipino attacks seized Ipo Dam intact. Further south, the 6th Division was relieved by the 38th Division, which ground away at the exhausted Japanese. Finally American persistance told, and the "*Shimbu*" Group's survivors began to melt away. Wawa Dam fell—also intact —on May 28, by which time the "*Shimbu*" Group had been destroyed.

By this time, too, the lesser problem of the "*Kembu*" Group, west of Clark Field, had also been solved. While the bulk of Griswold's corps prepared for the final advance on Manila at the end of January, the 40th Division had been left to mask the "*Kembu*" force of 25,000 in the heights to which it had retreated after the loss of Clark Field. Here, too, the Japanese made the fullest use of their advantage in terrain and it took over two months of concentrated pressure by three American divisions—first the 40th, then the 43rd, and finally the 38th—before Tsukada accepted the inevitable. On April 6 he ordered his surviving forces to go over to independent guerrilla warfare.

Two more Japanese concentrations south of Manila were also successfully broken up in these gruelling weeks. These were the "*Fuji*" Force commanded by Colonel Fujishige—an Army/Navy agglo-

meration of about 13,000 men, originally part of "*Shimbu*" Group–and 3,000 Army and Navy troops down on the Bicol Peninsula, the south-eastern "tail" of Luzon. Again, it was a story of repeated battles throughout February and March, with Filipino guerrillas working in co-ordination with the regular American forces. By the end of April "*Fuji*" Force had gone the same way as the "*Kembu*" Group, while an amphibious landing at Legaspi on the Bicol Peninsula by the 158th Regimental Combat Team had battered west and joined up with 1st Cavalry Division. Southern Luzon was free.

But the greatest obstacle of all remained: Yamashita and the 110,000 troops of the "*Shobu*" Group in the north. While the battles in the centre and south of Luzon continued, it was impossible for Krueger to send more than three divisions against Yamashita: the 33rd, 32nd, and 25th. Aided by the 37th Division, the 33rd pushed forward to take Baguio, Yamashita's former H.Q., on April 26; but it took the whole of May and June for Swift's I Corps to break across the Balete Pass, take Bambang, and push on into the Cagayan valley. Airborne forces were dropped at

◁△ *and* ◁◁ *Bombing Japanese air power into oblivion. Clark Field was under almost constant attack by both bombers and fighters. In both pictures "parafrag" bombs– fragmentation bombs released by parachute–can be seen hitting the airfield.*

△ *To be captured by the enemy was a worse fate than death, according to the Japanese military code of honour. When men of the 37th Infantry Division entered the town of Bayombong on Luzon, they found this hospital ward–with all the patients dead. Before evacuating the town, the Japanese had killed their own wounded rather than let them suffer the humiliation of falling into the hands of the enemy.*

◁ *American troops examine a Type 95 light tank, knocked out by tank destroyers.*

General MacArthur views the ruins in the Ermita district of Manila after U.S. forces cleared out the Japanese.
▷ △ Sherman tanks rumble past the Far Eastern University building – one of the few still relatively undamaged left standing in the city.
▷ ▽ The result of the tenacious defence put up by the Japanese in the streets of Manila – collapsing buildings and bodies hinder the work of American medical units.

the northern end of the Cagayan valley towards the end of June; they drove south and joined up with 37th Division at Tuguegarao on June 26.

By the end of June Yamashita had 65,000 men still under arms. They had been forced back into the mountains to the south of Bontoc and although it was now quite impossible for them to make any effective challenge to the American hold on Luzon, they nevertheless held out until the end of the war and kept four divisions tied down in consequence. Of all the Japanese forces told to hold the Philippines for the Emperor, Yamashita's men were the ones who came closest to fulfilling their mission.

Thus by the end of June 1945 the battle of Luzon was over. It had been a unique struggle, the most "European" battle of the entire Pacific war. Fought out on an island the size of Britain, it had seen tank battles, amphibious landings, paratroop drops and guerrilla warfare, with a bloody street battle as well. Japanese losses were immense, totalling around 190,000. Ameri-

The American Landing Ship, Medium (Rocket)

Displacement: 520 tons.
Armament: one 5-inch and two 40-mm
A.A. guns, four 4.2-inch mortars, and
85 to 105 5-inch rockets.
Speed: 12.5 knots.
Length: $203\frac{1}{2}$ feet.
Beam: $34\frac{1}{2}$ feet.
Draught: $7\frac{1}{4}$ feet.
Complement: 50.

The American Landing Ship, Tank

Displacement: 1,625 tons.
Armament: eight 40-mm A.A. guns (some
vessels had a 5-inch gun).
Speed: 11.6 knots.
Length: 328 feet.
Beam: 50 feet.
Draught: $11\frac{1}{4}$ feet.
Complement: 110.

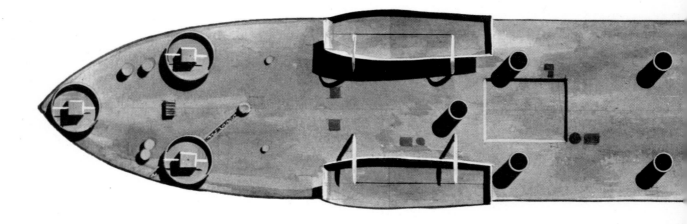

The American Landing Craft, Infantry (Large)

Displacement: 246 tons.
Armament: five 20-mm A.A. guns.
Speed: 14.4 knots.
Length: 159 feet.
Beam: $23\frac{3}{4}$ feet.
Draught: $5\frac{3}{4}$ feet.
Complement: 25.

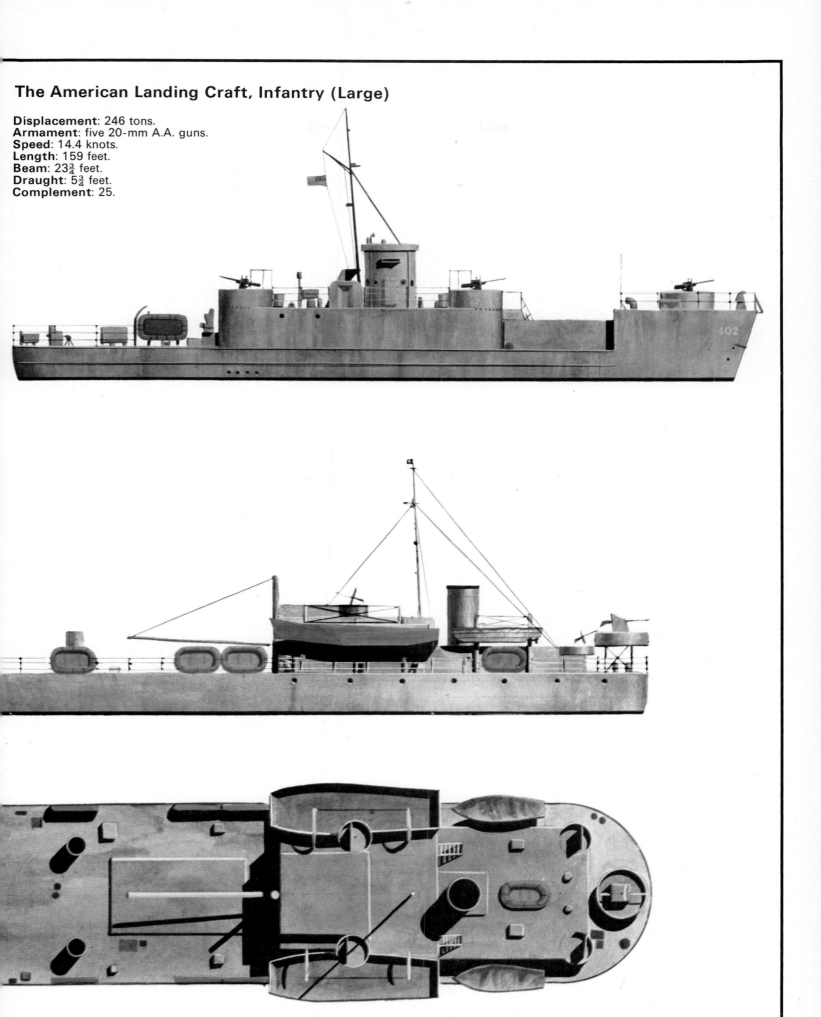

△ *The debris of war – three children huddle for shelter in the ruins of Manila. At least they survived to be cared for by the Americans – some 100,000 civilian residents of the city died.*

△▷ *An American poster designed to boost Filipino morale.*

can losses were 8,000 killed and 30,000 wounded. Further hard fighting lay ahead before the Pacific war would be brought to its close. But there would never be another conflict like the fight for Luzon.

MacArthur had never been ordered to liberate the entire Philippine archipelago. In fact, the British had been told by General Marshall that once the vital objectives had been secured in the Philippines, the liberation of the smaller islands would be left to the Filipinos themselves, with no major American forces taking part. But MacArthur had other ideas; and as long as it was clear that there were no other major objectives for the considerable American land, sea, and air forces in the Philippine area, he was allowed to have his way.

The clearing of the central and southern Philippines was entrusted to the U.S. 8th Army, under Lieutenant-General Robert L. Eichelberger, whose first task was to clear the short-cut sea route through the Visayan Passages. This began with a landing on the north-west coast of Samar on February 19 to clear the San Bernardino Strait and it continued through the month of March, with the occupation of small islands such as Burias, Siniara, Romblon, and Tablas. The last in the sequence was Masbate, and on April 5 Eichelberger reported to MacArthur that the Visayan Passages had been cleared.

In the meantime, the liberation of the key islands in the central and southern Philippines had already begun.

Eichelberger's opponent in the area was the commander of the Japanese 35th Army: Lieutenant-General Sosaku Suzuki. His forces numbered 100,000, dotted over scores of islands, unable to concentrate or assist each other, but prepared to put up as tenacious a fight as their colleagues on Luzon. And fight they did. By the middle of April Eichelberger's forces

THE FIGHTING FILIPINOS
...E WILL ALWAYS FIGHT FOR *FREEDOM!*

had made a grand total of 38 amphibious landings in the central and southern Philippines. None was on the same scale as Leyte or Luzon–but each met with resistance that was no less determined.

Palawan was the first major target: 270 miles long, the westernmost outrider of the Philippine archipelago. The American 186th Regimental Combat Team from the 41st Division landed on Palawan on February 28, but it took it over a week to break the resistance of the 1,750 Army and Navy troops on the island. On March 20 an airstrip at Puerto Princesa began to function.

Ten days before this, however, the rest of the 41st Division had descended on the westernmost tip of Mindanao, second largest and most southerly of the Philippine group. The long, thin Zamboanga Peninsula was their objective, but again it took over two weeks of fighting before their foothold was secure. In the meantime, 41st Division units had been detached to clean out the Sulu Archipelago, the string of diminutive islands stretched between Mindanao and Borneo. This

▽ *Clearing the Philippines and the recapture of the key areas in northern Borneo. This latter task was entrusted to the Australian I Corps under Lieutenant-General Sir Leslie Morshead. The Japanese had some 16 Army battalions and two Navy detachments of the 37th Army in the island. I Corps' naval support was furnished by the U.S. 7th Fleet. Although it had been planned to retake the whole of Borneo as a stepping stone towards Java, it was finally decided only to capture the oil producing areas and Brunei.*

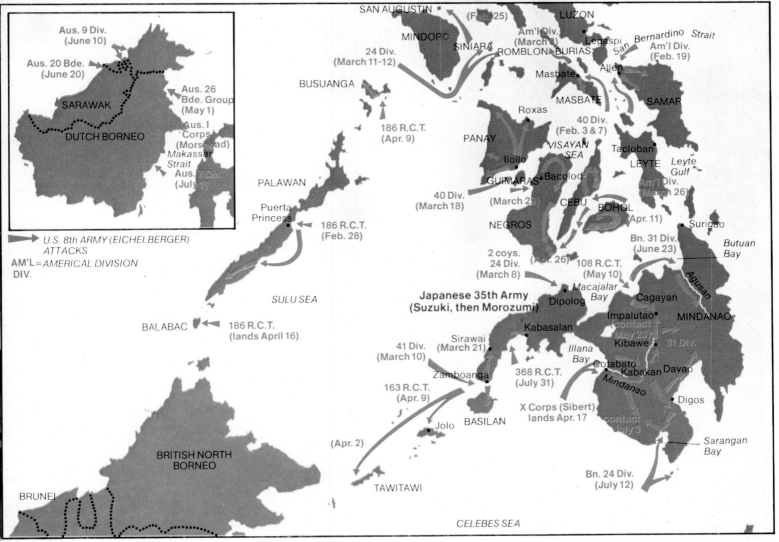

started easily – Basilan, nearest island in the Sulu group to Zamboanga, was un-occupied – but Jolo, in the centre of the chain, was another matter. It was held by 4,000 Japanese troops who fought hard for three weeks after the landing went in on April 9. Even after the main resistance was broken mopping-up continued in the interior of Jolo until July.

Next came the turn of the southern Visayas, four medium-sized islands on roughly the same latitude: from east to west, Bohol, Cebu, Negros, and Panay. Eichelberger divided this group into two, aided by the mountain spine of Negros which partitions the island into Negros Occidental and Negros Oriental. Panay and western Negros were given to the 40th Division; eastern Negros, Cebu, and Bohol to the Americal Division, originally raised in New Caledonia from non-divisional units in the Pacific theatre, and veterans of Guadalcanal, Bougainville, and Leyte.

The 40th Division landed on Panay on March 18 and wasted no time in complet-ing its assignment. It was consider-ably helped by strong guerrilla forces; they took Panay's largest port, Iloilo, on the 20th, crossed straight to the island of Guimaras, and landed on the western coast of Negros on March 29. Surprise had been their biggest ally to date, but awaiting them was the biggest Japan-ese force in the Visayas: 13,500 Army and air force troops commanded by Lieutenant-General Takeshi Kono. A prolonged battle lasted through April and May before Kono made the inevitable decision to take to the mountains. Over 6,000 of his men were still alive when the war ended.

By far the biggest fight in the Visayas fell to the Americal Division, which land-ed near Cebu City on March 26. There it found formidable defences, including mined beaches – an obstacle which 8th Army forces had not had to tackle before. A fortnight's hard fighting was needed to prise the Japanese out of their defences and start the mopping-up – but, once again, the Japanese were still holding out in June. In the meantime, Americal troops

had subdued Bohol in a mere two weeks after their landing on April 11, and had crossed to eastern Negros, where they joined 40th Division in hunting down the last 1,300 Japanese troops still on the run.

After the clearing of the Visayas and the Sulu Archipelago, only Mindanao remained: Mindanao, second largest island in the Philippines, and the island which MacArthur had originally planned to liberate first. It was a formidable obstacle. Suzuki had placed over half the 35th Army on Mindanao, intending to make the island the last bastion of Japanese resistance in the Philippines. He did not live to fight this last-ditch battle himself, as he was killed by American aircraft in April. His successor was Lieutenant-General Gyosaku Morozumi, who took over the 43,000 men of the garrison.

Despite the imposing size of their forces on Mindanao, the Japanese only controlled about five per cent of the island. The remainder was under the virtual control of the best equipped, organised, and led guerrilla forces in the Philippines, under the command of Colonel Wendell W. Fertig. The fact remained, however, that the Japanese held all the populated areas of Mindanao—hence MacArthur's determination to oust them.

The battle for Mindanao began on April 17, 1945, when General Sibert's X Corps landed at Illana Bay. Driving rapidly inland, Sibert's forces covered 115 miles in 15 days and pounced on Davao, depriving the Japanese of their last major town in the Philippines. Davao fell on May 3, but over a month of hard fighting in the hills of the interior lay ahead. Subsequent landings on the north coast of Mindanao, at Macalajar Bay and Butuan Bay, sent further American columns inland to split up the Japanese mass, which was not disrupted and forced into the jungle until the last week of June.

There remained some 2,000 Japanese in the extreme south of the island, who had been cut off there ever since Sibert's pounce on Davao in April-May. These fugitives were the objective of the last seaborne landing of the long struggle for the Philippines which had begun in Leyte Gulf in October 1944. On July 12 a battalion of the 24th Division went ashore to work with the local Filipino guerrillas in rounding up the Japanese. And they landed in Sarangani Bay, the southernmost inlet on Mindanao's coast. Once MacArthur had planned to launch the reconquest of the Philippines at this point. Instead it was the scene of the very last action in the campaign.

▽ *Crossing the Cagayan river beside the remains of a bridge blown by the Japanese. Men of the 139th Regiment, 37th Infantry Division, advance to attack Cagayan city.*

CHAPTER 164
The Pacific submarine war

by Richard Humble

▽ *An American submarine, one of the scourges of Japan's surface communications. Note the Goodyear "blimp" and the Sikorsky R-4 helicopter hovering overhead.*

△ *The Japanese submarine* I-53, *a Type KD3A boat. With a standard displacement of 1,635 tons and a torpedo armament of eight 21-inch tubes and 16 torpedoes, she was launched on August 8, 1925, completed on March 30, 1927, renumbered* I-153 *on May 5, 1942, surrendered to the Americans in 1945 and sunk in 1946.*

▽ *The Japanese submarine* I-68, *a Type KD6A boat. This type was capable of diving to 245 feet, had a standard displacement of 1,400 tons, and an armament of six 21-inch tubes and 14 torpedoes.* I-68 *was launched on June 26, 1933, completed on July 31, 1934, renumbered* I-168 *in May 1942, and sunk by the U.S. submarine* Scamp *on July 27, 1943.*

It is surprising that studies of the defeat of Imperial Japan in World War II rarely refer to the submarine war in the Pacific as the "Battle of the Pacific". Germany's failure to sever the Allied supply-routes across the Atlantic with her U-boats is well known, while the war beneath the sea on the other side of the world always seems to take second place to the dramatic battles fought on the surface. Yet, as General Hideki Tojo himself admitted to General MacArthur after Japan's surrender, there were three main reasons for the Allied victory in the Pacific. The first was the American ability to keep strong naval task forces at sea for months on end, supplying themselves as they went, without having to return to base. The second was the "leap-frogging" offensive which by-passed outlying Japanese garrisons and concentrated on targets of vital strategic importance. But the third was the virtual destruction of Japanese shipping by American submarines. This not only prevented Japan from conveying her

considerable reserves of manpower to the threatened sectors of her island empire. It also prevented her from supplying and reinforcing the troops already there.

As far as *matériel* was concerned, the Pacific war was a totally one-sided conflict, and this applied to the Japanese and U.S. submarine arms as to every other sphere. At the beginning, in December 1941, the opposing submarine forces in the Pacific were fairly well balanced with only a slight advantage to the Japanese. The Imperial Combined Fleet had 60 submarines, the U.S. Pacific Fleet 55. But a glance at the numbers of submarines built by both sides during World War II shows how completely this position was transformed. Between January 1942 and the end of the war the Japanese managed to launch 106 new submarine hulls. The Americans launched 204. And the other side of the coin—the numbers of submarines lost to enemy action and accidental causes—is even more revealing. Between Pearl Harbor and their surrender

the Japanese lost 125 submarines, the Americans only 54 – and it must be borne in mind that for the first 18 months after Pearl Harbor, until the Battle of the Atlantic was won in the summer of 1943, the U.S. Navy was fighting a two-ocean war.

These are the basic statistics of the submarine war in the Pacific theatre, and they show how completely the Japanese submarine arm was dwarfed by that of the U.S. Pacific Fleet by the end of the war. But when the Japanese Combined Fleet had launched its bid for instant victory in December 1941 its leaders had accepted that such a situation could only be expected from a long-term war with the United States. Far more serious was their failure to grasp the correct function of the submarine in modern war.

Like the tank, the submarine is an offensive weapon, forged to carry the assault home to the enemy. And if a fair comparison is to be drawn for the opposing submarine strategies used by the Americans and the Japanese in the Pacific, it may be

found in the radically different ways in which the Germans and the Western Allies employed their tanks in the campaign of 1940. The Panzers were massed into the "armoured wedge", the steel tip of the hurtling lance; the French and British still thought of the tank as the infantry support weapon *par excellence*. Even when the Allies did try to launch massed tank attacks before the final collapse came in the West, those attacks were essentially defensive, aimed at restoring stability to the shattered Allied front. So it was with the Pacific submarine war. By the last year of the war the American submariners were carrying out "wolf-pack" patrols as deadly as any undertaken by the German U-boat aces in their Atlantic heyday. The Japanese, however, had always cast their submarines in a defensive rôle.

There had been a time when this decision had seemed to make sense for the Japanese Navy. In 1922 the Washington naval limitation treaties had sought to

△ *The Japanese submarine* I-26, *a Type B1 boat. This boat was launched in 1940, completed on November 6, 1941. She was sunk off Leyte in October 1944.*

▽ *The Japanese submarine* I-176, *a Type KD7 boat. She was a boat of 1,630 tons' standard displacement, launched as* I-76 *in 1941, completed as* I-176 *on August 8, 1942, and sunk by the American destroyers* Franks, Haggard, *and* Johnston *on May 16, 1944.*

The American Consolidated PBY-5A patrol flying boat

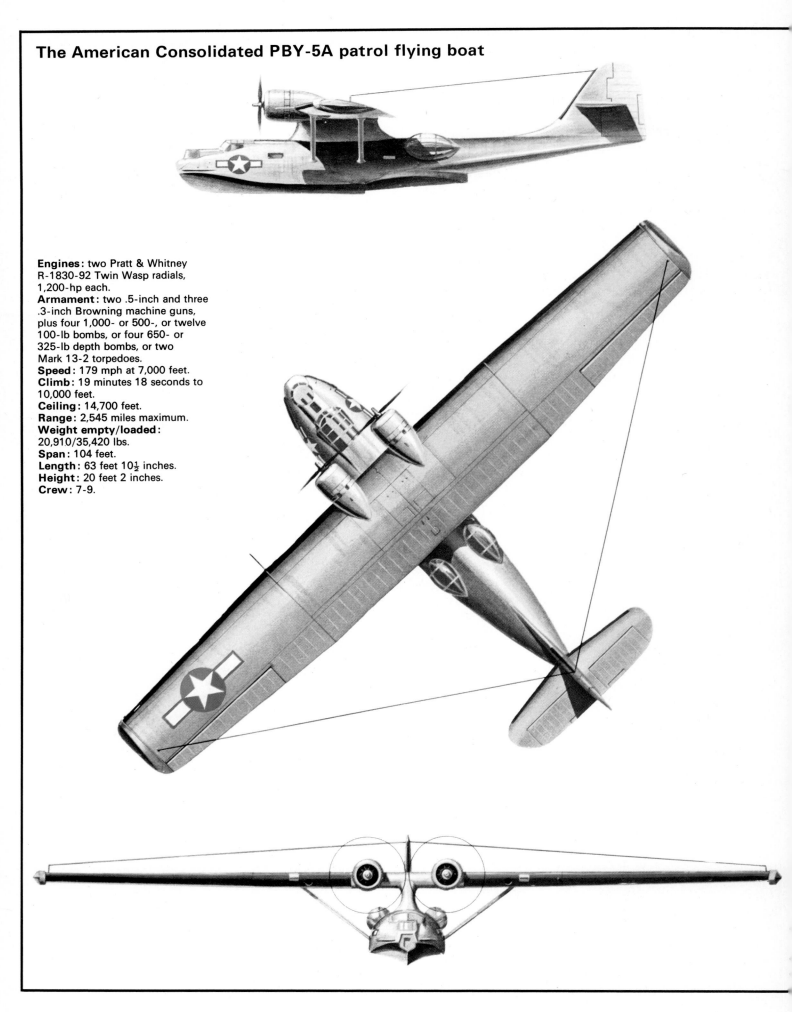

Engines: two Pratt & Whitney
R-1830-92 Twin Wasp radials,
1,200-hp each.
Armament: two .5-inch and three
.3-inch Browning machine guns,
plus four 1,000- or 500-, or twelve
100-lb bombs, or four 650- or
325-lb depth bombs, or two
Mark 13-2 torpedoes.
Speed: 179 mph at 7,000 feet.
Climb: 19 minutes 18 seconds to
10,000 feet.
Ceiling: 14,700 feet.
Range: 2,545 miles maximum.
Weight empty/loaded:
20,910/35,420 lbs.
Span: 104 feet.
Length: 63 feet 10½ inches.
Height: 20 feet 2 inches.
Crew: 7-9.

anticipate a new international warship-building race by "pegging" the strength ratios of the world's leading navies. This process had left Japan third in the league behind Britain and America. By that time it was perfectly obvious that the biggest naval rival whom Japan could expect to face in the event of any future war would be the United States and her Pacific Fleet based on the Hawaiian Islands. And it was the problem of tackling such a hypothetical threat with inferior numbers that gave birth to the defensive rôle of the Japanese submarine arm. As the U.S. Pacific Fleet steamed westward into Japanese waters, the Japanese submarines would launch repeated attacks, whittling down the American battle fleet until the Japanese surface fleet could meet it in battle on equal, if not superior, terms. But this was in the years before naval air power came into its own with the carrier task force. And it was based on an assumption which the events of World War I had already proved fallacious.

The tension of the Anglo-German naval building race in the years before 1914 had conditioned the world to expect that the coming of war would speedily result in a dreadnought Trafalgar between the opposing battle fleets. But this did not happen; and even when the battle fleets did clash at Jutland in 1916 it was a hideous accident for which the Germans had to compensate by running for home as best they could. For the Japanese in the first 12 months after Pearl Harbor, this anti-climactic situation was re-enacted. They could not entice the remnants of the U.S. Pacific Fleet to try the conclusion of a decisive action – and they had largely themselves to blame.

Ever since her defeat of the Russian fleet at Tsushima in 1905, Japan had been in the forefront of current naval development. Japan's new battle fleet had been equipped with some of the toughest warships in the world, and the Washington treaties had been expressly intended to prevent her from building even more formidable vessels. This forward thinking had lived on and had resulted in the Japanese aircraft-carrier building programme. But by the late 1930's it had been fatally compromised by the obsession with continued "super-battleship" construction – a paradoxical wedding of modernity and obsolescence. This meant that at the time of Pearl Harbor the Japanese Navy did not have a long-term carrier-building

programme, with results that have been abundantly described elsewhere in this history. And this "battleship obsession" kept the Japanese submarine arm from expanding into a purely offensive rôle.

Only limited successes

This is not to deny that the Japanese were capable of building good boats. During and after World War I they had studied the best (and worst) Western models and had drawn their own conclusions as to the optimum combination of speed, range, diving depth, and hitting-power. Of all the different types and modifications of submarine which the Japanese produced by the end of World War II, the Type B1 vessels may be taken as fairly typical of the Japanese fleet (as opposed to coastal defence) submarines. The B1 boats had a standard displacement of 2,198 tons, were capable of $23\frac{1}{2}$ knots on diesel and 8 knots on electric motors, had a cruising radius of 14,000 miles, and were possessed of an armament of one 5.5-inch gun, two 25-mm cannon, and six 21-inch torpedo tubes. They carried 17 torpedoes, plus a seaplane for extra reconnaissance range.

But these fleet submarines were ear-marked for scouting, not for strike-force duties. Again, the strategic importance of this scouting rôle was not lacking. Far from it. A classic example was Operation "K", on the eve of Midway. "K" envisaged the use of submarines as refuelling bases for long-range scout flying boats. Based on French Frigate Shoals, the submarines were supposed to refuel the flying boats before they made the last air reconnaissance of Pearl Harbor to check that the U.S. Pacific Fleet was there, duly waiting to be lured into the ambush at Midway. But "K" had to be abandoned. The three Japanese submarines – *I-121*, *I-122*, and *I-123* – found that the Americans had arrived at French Frigate Shoals themselves. Yamamoto did not get the information he needed to convert the strike at Midway into the final destruction of the U.S. Pacific Fleet, and his outer submarine patrol lines were thrown out of schedule by the setback. Nevertheless it fell to the submarine arm to win the biggest Japanese success at Midway, when Commander Tanabe of *I-168*, who had been reconnoitering Midway itself since the pre-

△ *Cramped accomodation on board an American submarine. Although first priority had to be given to the boat's armament and machinery, very careful thought was devoted to the problems of habitability, which had a considerable influence on crew performance, especially on long patrols.*

vious month, caught the immobilised carrier *Yorktown* with the destroyer *Hammann* lying alongside and sank them both with a salvo of four torpedoes.

After Midway the six-months' struggle for Guadalcanal ensued, and it was in this period that the Japanese submarine arm came the nearest it ever did to launching group operations against an enemy fleet. The intense sea fighting in the Guadalcanal area ran the full gamut from cruiser-destroyer clashes to carrier duels and battleship actions, with the balance constantly on a knife-edge. In August-September 1942, the Japanese submarine force kept the situation fluid by temporarily neutralising the American carrier strength in the South-West Pacific. On August 31 the *I-26* crippled the *Saratoga* so badly that she remained *hors de combat* for the next three months. A fortnight later the U.S. Pacific fleet suffered its first carrier loss since Midway, when *I-19* torpedoed the *Wasp* and

made an inferno of her. There was no chance of saving the blazing carrier and she was sunk by her own side. In the same attack other submarines blew the destroyer *O'Brien* out of the water and damaged the battleship *North Carolina* for good measure.

But that was the last real success scored by the Japanese submarine arm against the U.S. Pacific Fleet. The story of the next 18 months – Japan's defeat on Guadalcanal, the long fight for the Solomon islands chain, and the eventual loss of Bougainville – amounted to the grinding-down of Japan's magnificent night-fighting cruiser and destroyer crews in desperate attempts to supply their island garrisons. And while this was in progress a change had come over the planning of further additions to the Japanese submarine fleet.

In 1942 the last and biggest Japanese "attack" submarines – the giant "I-400" (Type STo) class – were ordered. These

▽ *The American submarine* Cuttlefish, *one of two units in the 1933 "Cachalot" class. She had a displacement of 1,130/ 1,650 tons, with speeds of 17/8 knots and an armament of one 3-inch gun and six 21-inch tubes (with 16 torpedoes). During the war the gun was moved to a position in front of the conning tower, and A.A. armament was increased considerably. She was scrapped in 1947.*

A Japanese merchantman meets her end and at the hands of a U.S. submarine in the wide reaches of the Pacific. The nature of Japan's outer perimeter, based on a series of small, scattered islands, without resources of their own, meant that Japan had to keep them supplied by means of a constant stream of ships. Thus the American submarines knew where to look for their prey; and their task was made the easier as Japan did not introduce a convoy system until late in the war. Even then, there were insufficient escort craft to give these small convoys much protection.

boats were the biggest submarines ever built by any power, and the plan was to use them to destroy the Pacific exit of the Panama Canal. *I-400* and her sister-ships had a standard displacement of 3,530 tons. Their overall length was $400\frac{1}{4}$ feet and their beam $39\frac{1}{3}$ feet. They could cruise 37,500 miles and dive to 325 feet, and their twin shafts were driven by four sets of diesels. They were so big that provision was made for camouflaging them with dummy funnels while cruising in home waters. Their armament was one 5.5-inch gun, ten 25-mm cannon (a sign that one of the biggest lessons of World War II, the danger of enemy air power, had not gone unlearned), and eight 21-inch torpedo tubes. Each of them could carry three specially-designed seaplane bombers, dismantled and stacked in huge, watertight hangars, plus torpedoes and bombs for them. What the "Yamato" class battleships were to the surface fleet, the I-400's were to the submarine arm. But both ideas were based on fatal misconceptions. There was no point in building giant battleships if there were not enough carriers to keep off enemy aircraft. And there was no target which could possibly justify the construction of the I-400's–not even the Panama Canal, which was not the only way the Allies could move up supplies for their fleets in the Pacific. As examples of how big submarines could be built, the I-400's stood

alone. But they were white elephants Only three of them were completed (*I-400 I-401*, and *I-402*). None of them was ready for service before 1945 (*I-402* was no completed until July of that year). Oddly enough all three survived the massive American bombing of Japan's naval bases and surrendered–to be sunk by the Americans in 1946.

Useless fanaticism

The three I-400's are a perfect example of Santayana's dictum that fanaticism consists of redoubling your efforts when you have forgotten your aim. Admiral Dönitz and his U-boat flotillas not only had a good chance of strangling the British Isles by striking at their supply-routes: the U-boats came perilously close to doing so. Japan, on the other hand, could hardly even begin to embarrass the North American continent by submarine attacks. It is not so much a question of looking back with the benefit of hindsight and stating what the Japanese Navy should have done with its submarines What could it have done?

A concentration of long-range fleet submarines could have seriously embarrassed America's direct sealane from the West Coast to Pearl Harbor–but this would only have made sense in the

The American Northrop P-61B Black Widow night-fighter and intruder

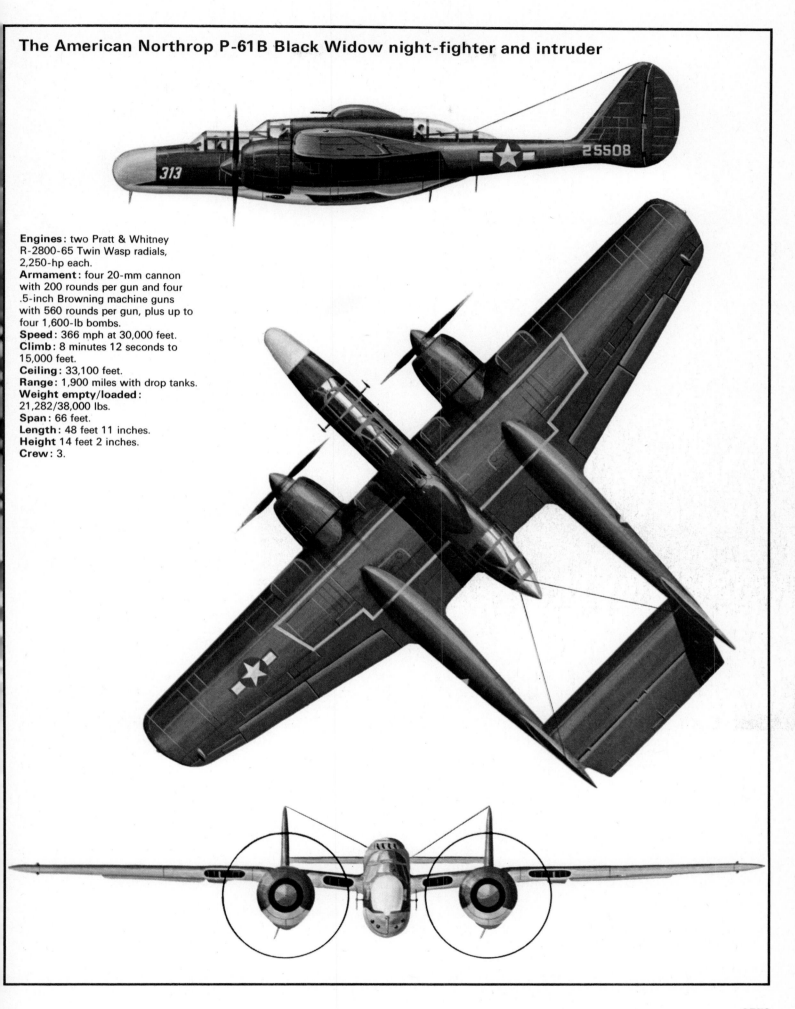

Engines: two Pratt & Whitney
R-2800-65 Twin Wasp radials,
2,250-hp each.
Armament: four 20-mm cannon
with 200 rounds per gun and four
.5-inch Browning machine guns
with 560 rounds per gun, plus up to
four 1,600-lb bombs.
Speed: 366 mph at 30,000 feet.
Climb: 8 minutes 12 seconds to
15,000 feet.
Ceiling: 33,100 feet.
Range: 1,900 miles with drop tanks.
Weight empty/loaded:
21,282/38,000 lbs.
Span: 66 feet.
Length: 48 feet 11 inches.
Height 14 feet 2 inches.
Crew: 3.

△ *The end of two more Japanese cargo vessels, seen through the graticule of their sinker's periscope.*

months before Midway. After June 1942 the centre of gravity of the naval war in the Pacific shifted to the South-West Pacific, and that was where the Japanese submarines could have done most damage. Although the range of the best Japanese fleet submarines was great, it was not great enough – and there were not enough of them – to have begun to be a serious threat to the West Coast-Pearl Harbor route and to the New Zealand-South Pacific-Australia route.

The successes achieved by the Japanese submarines during the sea fight for Guadalcanal give a clue as to the best submarine strategy which Japan could have followed after the initiative was lost in the Solomons: biding her time, and committing strong submarine flotillas to gnaw at the American task forces once the target of their next attack had been definitely pinpointed and that attack committed. Instead the Japanese fleet commanders fell into the trap of fighting attrition battles with their surface forces;

and in these battles they lost so heavily (the equivalent of an entire peace-time fleet was sunk at Guadalcanal) that the submarine force was headed in another direction. The Solomons campaign proved decisively that running in supplies on the surface by night was futile and extravagant. Submarines must therefore be used for the job in future battles.

This was a compound error. First, the American "leap-frogging" island strategy asked for nothing better than that the Japanese should dissipate their efforts in trying to supply by-passed island garrisons. And second, the building of supply submarines and the conversion of existing boats for supply duties only drew more teeth from the already ineffective Japanese submarine force.

As it was, the supply rôle forced on the submarine programme produced the Type D1 boats. No less than 12 of them were built, with numbers running from *I-361* to *I-372*. The emphasis was on stowage and range. They carried no torpedoes but retained the standard 5.5-inch gun and two 25-mm cannon. The D1 boats had an endurance of 60 days; they could cruise 15,000 miles on the surface and had an extremely generous submerged cruising radius of 120 miles, conferred by the fitting of extra batteries. They could carry up to 82 tons of supplies plus 110 troops, and on their outer casings they could carry two 42-foot landing-craft. To help land supplies at journey's end, two big inflatable rubber rafts were also included. These 12 submarines were all launched during 1944, the last of them, *I-372*, on November 8. Not one of them could have threatened so much as an American destroyer. And their respective fates speak for themselves:

I-361: Sunk by carrier aircraft 400 miles south-east of Okinawa, May 30, 1945.

I-362: Sunk by U.S.S. *Fleming* (destroyer escort) 320 miles north-north-east of Truk, January 18, 1945.

I-363: Mined off Kyūshū, October 29, 1945.

I-364: Torpedoed by U.S.S. *Sea Devil* (submarine) 300 miles east-south-east of Yokosuka, September 16, 1944.

I-365: Torpedoed by U.S.S. *Scabbardfish* (submarine) 75 miles south-east of Yokosuka, November 28, 1944.

I-366: Survived. Surrendered to U.S. Navy and sunk (with the bulk of the captured Japanese submarines), April 1946.

I-367: Survived. Surrendered to U.S. Navy and sunk (with the bulk of the captured Japanese submarines), April 1946.

I-368: Sunk by carrier aircraft, 35 miles west of Iwo Jima, February 27, 1945.

I-369: Survived. Surrendered and scrapped in U.S.A.

I-370: Sunk by U.S.S. *Finnegan* (destroyer escort) 120 miles south of Iwo Jima, February 26, 1945.

I-371: Torpedoed by U.S.S. *Lagarto* (submarine) in the Bungo Straits, February 24, 1945.

I-372: Sunk by carrier aircraft at Yokosuka, July 18, 1945.

These melancholy figures show the appalling wastage of the Japanese submarine force in the closing months of the war. But one further bizarre refinement lay in store for Japan's submarines. This was part and parcel of the *kamikaze* programme as it affected the Navy, and it involved the modification of submarines to carry *Kaiten* (one-man suicide torpedoes).

At the beginning of the war the Japanese submariners had placed great hopes in their midget submarines, which also had to be carried to within range of the target by parent ships. These attacks had nearly all ended in fiasco; and the *Kaiten*

▽ *An American submarine commander lines up his prey. Note the men at the diving plane controls in the background.*

programme at the end of the war was little better. It was the logical development of the myopia and strategic misapprehensions which had bedevilled the Imperial Japanese submarine force throughout the war.

It is necessary to catalogue the mistakes which rendered the Japanese submarine arm virtually impotent, simply because they are matched by such a totally different story in the American camp. Even by the end of the Pacific war, the American submarine force in the Pacific was only a tiny fraction of the total American naval strength in the theatre: a mere two per cent. Yet that two per cent achieved one of the biggest feats in naval history.

equipped by sea. Yet the Japanese, for all the matchless fighting tradition of their Navy, committed one of the most appalling blunders in naval history–one which, as Tojo admitted, helped lose them the war– in failing to safeguard their mercantile shipping.

They did not sail their ships in convoy; and they did not, in consequence, develop any effective anti-submarine techniques. The result was a gift for the aggressive American submariners, who ended the war being credited with the destruction of 63 per cent of Japanese shipping. When itemised, this percentage is seen to be made up of 1,152 Japanese merchantmen of over 500 tons, a total of 4,861,317 gross tons. And the bulk of these sinkings was

△ Kairyu *suicide craft photographed in Yokosuka after the end of the war. The type was based loosely on the Type A midget submarine, and the first prototype was built late in 1943. Full scale production got under way in February 1945, and by the end of the war 215 had been completed (207 at Yokosuka), and another 207 were building. The type displaced 19¼ tons submerged, had a diving depth of 330 feet and a submerged range of 36 miles at 3 knots, and an armament of two 18-inch torpedoes or a 1,320-lb charge in the nose. Two crew were carried.*

Once the desperate situation of summer 1942 had been retrieved for the U.S. Pacific Fleet by Midway, conditions were ripe for its submarine force to go into action on the offensive. And everything was on the U.S. side.

If we agree that the Japanese made fatal mistakes in the basic use of their own submarines, it must be concluded that these were nothing to the errors made in safeguarding their own shipping from enemy submarine attacks. The victories won by the Japanese down to Coral Sea and Midway had given them an empire consisting of the western half of the Pacific Ocean, punctuated by dots of land. It was a sea empire, whose "provinces" could only be supplied and

the work of the American submarines alone. The British and Dutch submarines operating out of the Indian Ocean also drew blood, but their credited "kills" only made up about two per cent of the total.

The U.S. Navy was fortunate that when it went to war its submarine arm was already scheduled to receive one of the most successful "production-line" class of warship ever produced: the "Gato" class submarines.

These boats displaced 1,525/2,415 tons, with a waterline length of 307 feet; they could make 20¼ knots on diesel and 10 knots on electric motors. Their armament concentrated on the submarine's main punch: torpedoes. They carried ten 21-

inch tubes (two more, be it noted, than the gross Japanese I-400's. In addition they had a 5-inch gun and a 40-mm quick-firer. A total of 200 Gato's had been launched by the time of the Japanese surrender, and 27 "Tench" class boats, the latter being improved Gato's. It is significant, as an indication of the fantastic output of the United States' warship-building programme, that all these submarines were produced from the same number of yards as the Japanese possessed. America's submarines as totalled above came from the yards of Manitowoc, Mare Island, Electric Boat, Portsmouth, Cramp, and Boston; Japan's from Kure, Sasebo, Mitsubishi, Yokosuka, and the two Kawasaki yards at Kobe and Senshu.

It is interesting that in the beginning the American submariners were bedevilled by the same defect which limited the early successes of the U-boat commanders of World War II: faulty torpedoes. They tended to run too deep and suffer from temperamental magnetic pistols. (The Japanese, by comparison, had the decisive upper hand in torpedoes with their oxygen-propelled "Long Lance", used to such deadly effect by their surface ships in the Battle of the Java Sea and in the Solomons battles.) This, however, did not prevent them from wreaking havoc among the isolated Japanese merchantmen. Top-scoring submarine of the "Gato" class boats was *Flasher,* which sank 21 ships totalling 100,231 tons; four others of the same class—*Rasher, Tang, Silversides,* and *Barb*—all managed to score total "kills" of over 90,000 tons.

American tactics were far more aggressive than those of their opposite numbers. One obvious reason for this was the invaluable aid of radar—both air-search and surface-search—which began to be installed in American submarines from 1942. But in general the Japanese produced few enterprising submarine commanders of the calibre of Commander Tanabe of *I-168,* who evaded destruction at Midway by diving into his own diesel smoke and hiding under the American destroyers searching for him. The Americans, on the other hand, produced commanders who became adept at the daring "down the throat" shot—surfacing directly ahead of a charging enemy and torpedoing head on. Slightly less hair-raising was the "up the kilt" shot from astern.

The losses of the Japanese D1 boats quoted above contain other evidence.

Three of the sunk boats were the victims of American submarines; two were sunk by American escort destroyers, by 1944 and 1945 an essential part of the carrier task force's screen. Certainly the biggest "kill" scored in a single American submarine attack came on November 29, 1944, when *Archerfish* put four torpedoes into the giant new carrier *Shinano* and sank her off the Japanese coast.

Such, in outline, is the unsung story of the submarine war in the Pacific, which played so great a part in the defeat of Japan. On the Japanese side there was a confused and short-sighted blend of the old and the new; on the other there was unchallengeable technical superiority, wielded by masters of their trade.

△ *The end of the road for the depleted remnants of Japan's submarine striking force: the I-400, I-401,* and *I-14 (left to right) moored alongside the U.S. submarine tender* Proteus. *I-400 and I-401 were sister ships and are described in the text, and I-14 was one of four Type AM units: I-1 and I-15 were not completed, I-13 was sunk on December 16, 1944, and I-14 was surrendered at sea. The boats of this class had a displacement of 4,762 tons submerged, low speeds of $16\frac{3}{4}/5\frac{1}{2}$ knots, and an armament of one 5.5-inch and seven 25-mm guns, plus six 21-tubes (12 torpedoes) and two seaplanes.*

The American submarine *Ray*

Displacement: 1,526/2,424 tons.
Armament: one 5-inch, one
40-mm A.A., two .5-inch A.A.,
and two .3-inch A.A. guns, plus ten
21-inch torpedo tubes and 24
torpedoes.
Speed: $20\frac{1}{4}/8\frac{3}{4}$ knots.
Diving depth: 300 feet.
Length: $311\frac{3}{4}$ feet.
Beam: $27\frac{1}{4}$ feet.
Draught: $15\frac{1}{4}$ feet.
Complement: 85.

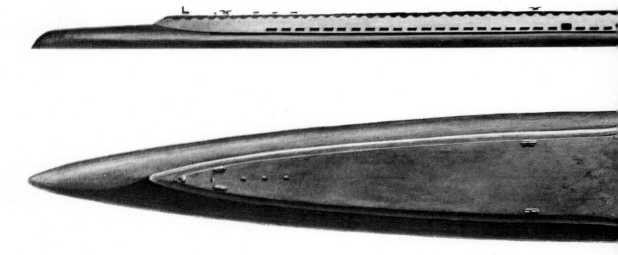

The Japanese submarine *I-400*

Displacement: 5,223/6,560 tons.
Armament: one 5.5-inch and ten
25-mm guns, plus eight 21-inch
torpedo tubes and three seaplanes.
Speed: $18\frac{3}{4}/6\frac{1}{2}$ knots.
Radius: 30,000 miles at 16 knots/
60 miles at 3 knots.
Length: $400\frac{1}{4}$ feet.
Beam: $39\frac{1}{3}$ feet.
Draught: 23 feet.
Complement: 144.

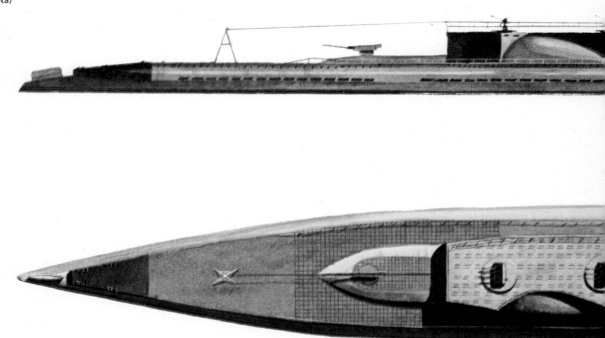

CHAPTER 165
The British Pacific Fleet

by Captain Donald Macintyre

The crucial Allied agreement on how World War II should be conducted was that the war in the Pacific should be subordinated to the defeat of Germany. Nevertheless, when the naval war in European waters had turned decisively in favour of the Allies in September 1943 with the defeat of the U-boat campaign in the Atlantic and the elimination of the Italian fleet in the Mediterranean, Winston Churchill at once offered to President Roosevelt to send a squadron to the Pacific.

The motive behind this offer was two-fold. There was a genuine desire to repay the generous assistance Britain had received from the United States; there was also the need to restore British prestige in the Orient by sharing in the defeat of Japan. A distinct lack of enthusiasm with which this proposal was regarded by the all-powerful head of the U.S. Navy, Admiral Ernest J. King, had a similarly complex source. King's single-minded

▽ *Fleet Air Arm Corsair fighters on the hangar deck of a carrier of the British Pacific Fleet. Note the variation on the ordinary roundel, with the red centre deleted to avoid confusion with the Japanese* hinomaru *or* "meatball" *markings.*

devotion to the Navy he served was coloured by a widely-felt and long-standing jealousy of the Royal Navy's erstwhile domination of the oceans of the world. He was determined that its eclipse behind the newly arisen sea power of the United States should be permanent. At the same time he was convinced that the Royal Navy, experienced in and trained and equipped for the relatively short-range warfare in European and Atlantic waters, could not be re-shaped and re-equipped in time to fight effectively in the vast spaces of the Pacific.

King correctly appreciated that the British would find it very difficult to build up the essential logistic organisation. Apart from the establishment of huge stocks of stores and equipment at a main base—in this case Sydney, N.S.W., many thousands of miles from their source—it required the onward transport of such supplies via an advanced base, a further 2,000 miles (in the event it was to be 3,500 miles) to the operational area. In fact, a huge fleet of repair ships, store carriers, ferry carriers, ammunition ships, fast tankers, amenity ships, harbour service craft, the whole known as the "Fleet Train", would have to be procured. The majority of these would be merchant ships. And as, by an early agreement when the United States entered the war, the building of standard merchant ships had been made exclusively a task for American shipyards, while British yards concentrated mainly on warships, and as British merchantmen were for the most part worn out by five hard years of war, ships of the Fleet Train would have to come mainly out of the American building programme.

Nevertheless, by September 1944, Churchill, when offering to place the British main fleet under United States supreme command to operate against the Japanese in the Pacific, felt able to state that an adequate Fleet Train had been assembled. In November of that year the British Pacific Fleet was formed at Colombo with Admiral Sir Bruce Fraser as its Commander-in-Chief. It was to be centred upon a squadron under Rear-Admiral Sir Philip Vian, composed of the fleet carriers *Indefatigable, Illustrious,*

Victorious, and *Indomitable,* to be joined later by the *Formidable* and *Implacable.*

Designed in 1936 with the possibility of war with Germany and Italy in mind, and the likelihood of having to operate within range of superior, shore-based air forces, these ships incorporated a thickly-armoured flight-deck. In the first four to be built this restricted them to a single hangar and to an aircraft complement of about 50, as compared with the 100 aircraft in two hangars in the U.S.S. *Essex* and her numerous sisters, where the flight deck was a light structure with a wooden deck. The *Indefatigable* and *Implacable* were modified to give them an extra half-hangar and a complement of 72 aircraft. British battleships, an essential part of any carrier task force, were slower than American contemporaries.

By this stage of the war a programme of re-equipment of the Fleet Air Arm with American types of carrier aircraft–Hellcat and Corsair fighters and Avenger torpedo-bombers–was in progress. These were to take the place of the Seafires and Sea Hurricanes, unsuitable adaptations of R.A.F. fighters, and the unsuccessful Barracuda torpedo-bombers which were all that the British aircraft industry had been

able to provide. Not only did the British aircraft lack the robustness necessary for deck operation, but their fuel endurance was also less than that of American types. Unfortunately only four of the carriers were to be re-equipped before the B.P.F. joined the 5th Fleet–with consequences which will be discussed later. An escort of battleships, cruisers, and destroyers would support the carriers. As Fraser would be too senior to serve directly under an American fleet commander, he was to fly his flag ashore while Vice-Admiral Sir Bernard Rawlings with his flag in the battleship *King George V* would command the British Pacific Fleet at sea.

This fleet, based on Colombo, was steadily built up and trained through the autumn and winter of 1944. It was "blooded" and trained in a series of carrier strike operations directed at the Japanese-held oil installations in Sumatra and Java. The new methods and tempo of carrier operations which had been evolved in the Pacific War were exercised; and when the fleet reached Sydney on February 10, 1945, it felt ready to operate alongside the U.S. 5th Fleet in the current operations to capture Okinawa. Whether this could be effectively done, however, was

△ *The battleship* Howe *passes through the Suez Canal en route to the Far East.*

◁ and ▷ *Carrier operations.*
▽ *Resupply at sea for a British destroyer. One of the main disadvantages under which the B.P.F. had to operate was the inadequacy of its Supply Train of depot ships and auxiliaries.*

to depend to a crucial degree upon how ready the Fleet Train was to give its essential support. When the B.P.F. moved forward to the advanced base of Manus in the Admiralty Islands, it was to be sadly disappointed in this respect. Out of 69 ships earmarked for the Fleet Train, only 27 had arrived, many of the remainder having been delayed by the chronic labour troubles of the Sydney water-front.

Under these conditions and in the humid heat of a climate for which the British warships were ill-adapted, it was deeply disappointing to be delayed because of an apparently continuing unwillingness of the American allies to welcome them. Admiral King, knowing the B.P.F.'s logistic weakness, was still holding out for it to be used as part of the U.S. 7th Fleet in General MacArthur's South-West Pacific Command in the less-sophisticated naval task involved in the re-conquest of Borneo. Not until March 18 were his objections overborne and, under orders to form part of the U.S. 5th Fleet, the British force sailed from Manus as Task Force 57 on the 23rd. Admiral Vian commanded the carrier squadron with his flag in the 23,000-ton *Indomitable*.

The aircraft complement of the four carriers was as follows:

	Fighters	Bombers
Indefatigable	40 Seafires	20 Avengers
	9 Fireflies	
Illustrious	36 Corsairs	16 Avengers
Indomitable	29 Hellcats	15 Avengers
Victorious	37 Hellcats	14 Avengers

Though the B.P.F. was nominally a Task Force, it was less than equivalent to one of the four Task Groups of which Task Force 58, the 5th Fleet's carrier element, was composed. It was placed under the command of the C.-in-C. 5th Fleet, Admiral Spruance, but its tactical control was reserved to Admiral Rawlings. Combined with the well-founded doubts of the Americans that the less-experienced and, in some ways, less well-equipped British carriers, their speed restricted by the comparatively slow escorting battleships, could operate effectively in close conjunction with their own Task Groups, this resulted in the British force operating at this time independently and against a separate complex of targets. While the main body of the 5th Fleet operated in direct support of the assault on Okinawa, the B.P.F. struck at airfields in the Sakashima group of islands to the southward, which the Japanese used as staging points for their aircraft.

The first strike was flown off at sunrise on March 26, 1945, when 60 Corsairs and Hellcats and 24 Avengers attacked air-

◁ *Preparing for a mission on board a British carrier operating in the Pacific.*
△ *Grumman Avenger torpedo-bombers off on a strike.*

The British battleship *Howe*

Displacement: 35,000 tons.
Armament: ten 14-inch, sixteen 5.25-inch
A.A., eighty-eight 2-pdr, eight 40-mm A.A.,
and sixteen 20-mm A.A., guns, plus 4 aircraft.
Armour: $4\frac{1}{2}$- to 15-inch belt, 1- to 6-inch
deck, 9- to 16-inch turrets, and 16-inch
control tower.
Speed: 29 knots.
Length: 745 feet.
Beam: 103 feet.
Draught: $27\frac{3}{4}$ feet.
Complement: 1,558.

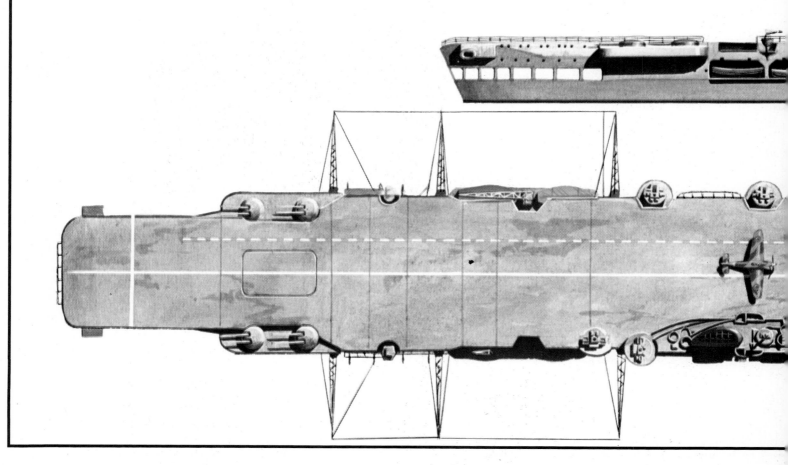

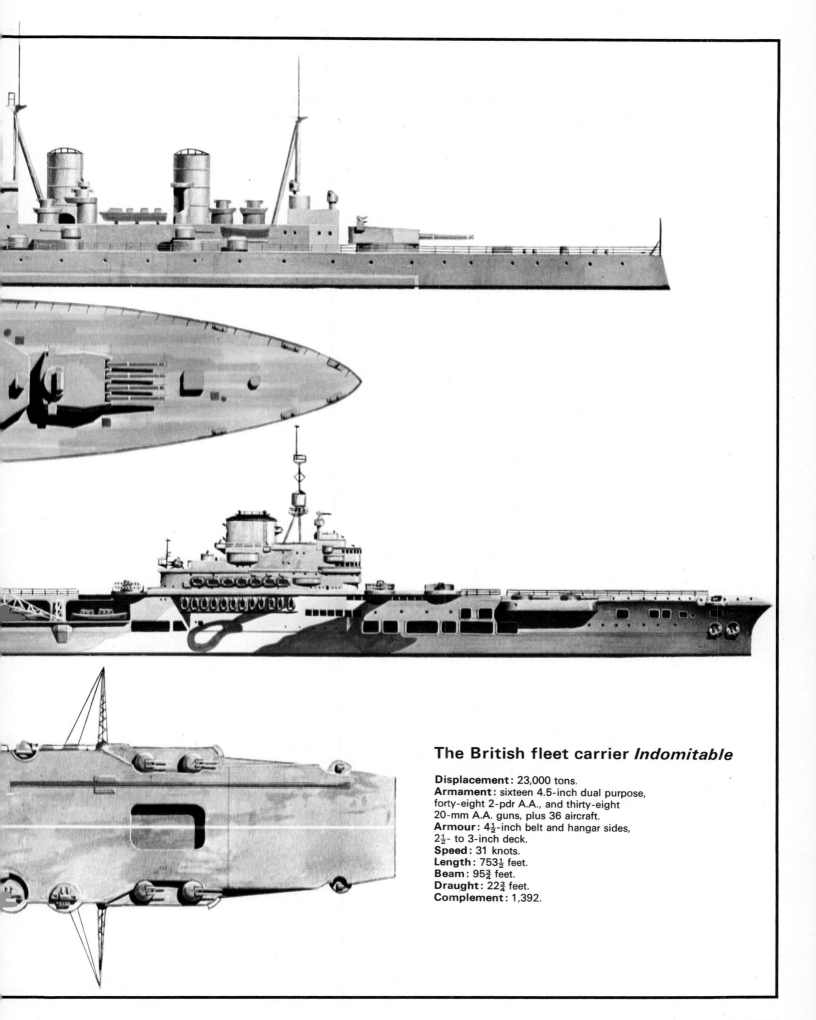

The British fleet carrier *Indomitable*

Displacement: 23,000 tons.
Armament: sixteen 4.5-inch dual purpose,
forty-eight 2-pdr A.A., and thirty-eight
20-mm A.A. guns, plus 36 aircraft.
Armour: 4½-inch belt and hangar sides,
2½- to 3-inch deck.
Speed: 31 knots.
Length: 753½ feet.
Beam: 95¾ feet.
Draught: 22¾ feet.
Complement: 1,392.

fields on Miyako Island. Seafires, on account of their poor endurance, were kept airborne over the fleet as Combat Air Patrol; they were to be restricted to this defensive rôle throughout the campaign. With two-day intervals for refuelling at sea (when the lack of experience in all concerned and the unreliable equipment and methods employed were exposed) similar strikes were repeated over the next 26 days.

The targets allocated had proved disappointing; few enemy aircraft were encountered, while the coral airfield runways, cratered during the day, were repaired each night before daylight. On the other hand the ground defences were far from negligible and a number of carrier planes were shot down. And on April 1 the B.P.F. had its first experience of attack by Japanese suicide planes—the *kamikaze*. Early that morning one of these broke through the fighter defence to crash and explode against the base of the *Indefatigable*'s island, killing 14 men and injuring 16 more. The armoured flight

deck now justified itself, preventing crippling damage; within a few hours the ship was again operational. In a second attack on the 6th, this time on the *Illustrious*, the suicide bomber just failed to hit the flight deck, though its wing actually struck the carrier's superstructure as it crashed alongside.

The several *kamikaze* attempts on that day, of which this came nearest to success, were only the back-wash of the first massed attack, or *kikusui*, by some 355 *kamikaze* planes and an equal number of normal bombers on the 5th Fleet. Their attack fell chiefly on the air warning pickets of destroyers maintained at a distance from the fleet. Three of these were sunk as well as three destroyers of the circular screen round the carriers; 18 more were damaged. Other *kikusui* attacks were to follow and would continue until well into June. In that period no less than 27 ships were to be sunk by suicide attacks and 164 damaged, including several American carriers, whose unarmoured flight decks made them very

▽ *Bombs burst along a runway on Ishagaki Island in the Sakishima group during a British carrier strike intended to draw Japanese reinforcements away from the landings on Okinawa.*

The British Supermarine Seafire III fighter

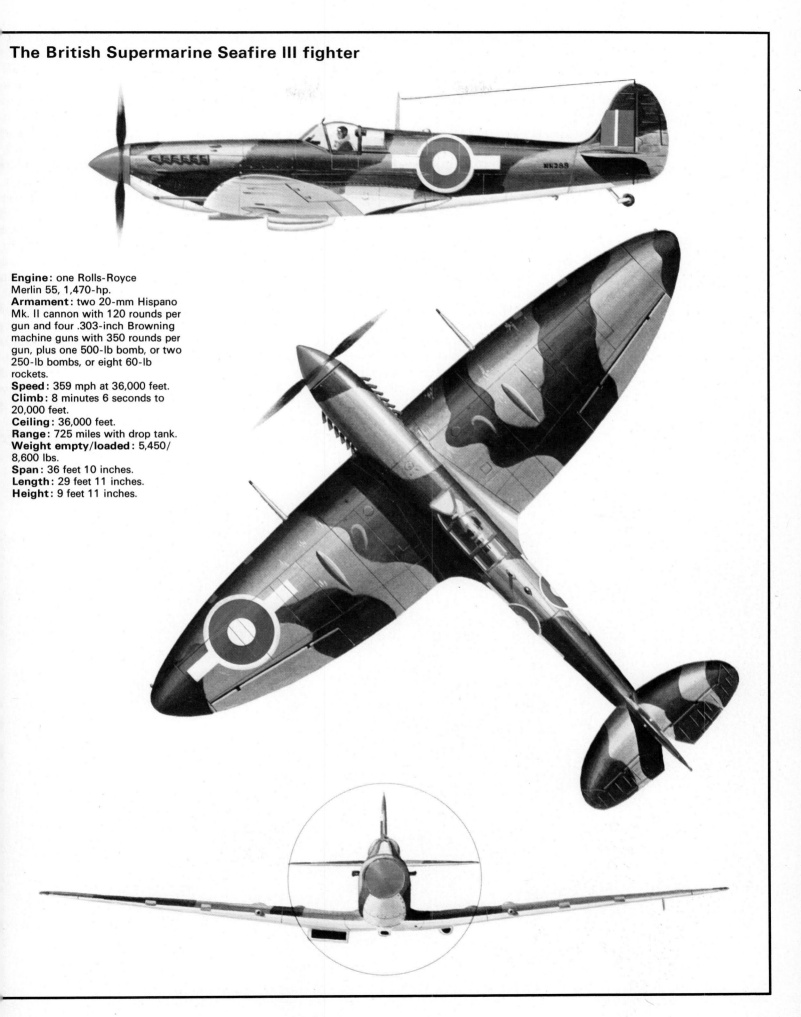

Engine: one Rolls-Royce Merlin 55, 1,470-hp.
Armament: two 20-mm Hispano Mk. II cannon with 120 rounds per gun and four .303-inch Browning machine guns with 350 rounds per gun, plus one 500-lb bomb, or two 250-lb bombs, or eight 60-lb rockets.
Speed: 359 mph at 36,000 feet.
Climb: 8 minutes 6 seconds to 20,000 feet.
Ceiling: 36,000 feet.
Range: 725 miles with drop tank.
Weight empty/loaded: 5,450/ 8,600 lbs.
Span: 36 feet 10 inches.
Length: 29 feet 11 inches.
Height: 9 feet 11 inches.

vulnerable. As early as the second week in April the American C.-in-C. was having to consider withdrawal of the fleet from the operations.

To assist his defence arrangements, the B.P.F.'s targets were switched on April 12 and 13 to airfields in the northern part of Formosa whence it was believed that many of the most experienced enemy attacks were coming. The raids were successful, with 16 Japanese planes shot down for the loss of only three British. They drew down on the British carriers some determined attacks in return, all of which were defeated by fighters of the C.A.P. or shot down by gunfire. The first period of duty for the B.P.F. should have ended on the 13th, but to relieve the pressure on the 5th Fleet from the massed attacks which went on throughout the 14th, Admiral Rawlings offered to return for a further period after refuelling on the 14th and 15th, an offer which was readily accepted. Finally, on April 20, after gathering in the last returning aircraft, the B.P.F. shaped course for San Pedro Bay, Leyte, for a brief period of rest and replenishment.

▽ *Firefighters at work after a kamikaze has crashed onto a British carrier. It was in such circumstances that the armoured flight decks of the British fleet carriers proved their worth.*

There the *Formidable*, carrying six Hellcat and 36 Corsair fighters and 12 Avengers, joined to replace the *Illustrious,* which was by this time in need of a refit and whose fighter squadrons had passed the accepted limit for an operational tour of duty. And on May 1 the B.P.F. sailed again to resume the task of neutralising the Sakishima airfields. Nothing has been said up to now about the two battleships, five cruisers, and 11 destroyers of the fleet. Their functions were almost entirely in support of the carrier squadron, the battleships and cruisers with their anti-aircraft gunfire, the destroyers to guard against submarine attack (which in fact never materialised) and to act as distant air-warning pickets to back up the overcrowded radar information. Now, however, on May 4, Admiral Rawlings brought some fresh interest into the lives of the larger ships by taking the battleships *King George V* and *Howe* and his cruisers to bombard the airfields on Miyako.

While this large proportion of the fleet's anti-aircraft gunnery strength was away, a *kamikaze* attack managed to evade the C.A.P. A Zero fighter and its bombs

crashed onto the *Formidable,* holing even her stout armoured flight deck: splinters penetrated the ship's central boiler room and her speed was reduced to 18 knots. Eight men were killed and 47 more injured. Eleven aircraft on deck were destroyed. Yet within 90 minutes the *Formidable* was living up to her name, steaming at 24 knots and operating her aircraft. During the same attack another suicide pilot had attempted to do the same to the *Indomitable* but bounced over the side before his bomb exploded, doing only minor damage. Until May 25 Task Force 57 repeated its previous operational pattern with two days delivering strikes on enemy airfields followed by two days of replenishment.

On May 9 the *Formidable* was hit again squarely on her flight deck in the middle of her parked aircraft, 18 of which were destroyed. But 50 minutes later she was ready to operate aircraft. At about the same time a *kamikaze* exploded near the forward lift of the *Victorious.* The deck was holed and a serious fire started. Two minutes later a second bomber crashed the ship but bounced over the side before exploding. The *Victorious* was only out of action for a short while. But both she and the *Formidable* had lost so many aircraft that they had to withdraw for three days to rendezvous with a ferry carrier of the Fleet Train and embark more.

The last strikes by British planes in the Okinawa campaign were delivered on May 25, after which Task Force 57 shaped course for Sydney for repairs and recreation in preparation for the coming assault on the Japanese homeland. As the *Indomitable* was in need of a refit, her place was to be taken by the newly arrived *Implacable,* whose aircraft complement was 48 Seafires, 12 Fireflies, and 15 Avengers. Admiral Vian shifted his flag to the *Formidable.* While the remainder of the fleet was at Sydney, the *Implacable* and three newly-joined cruisers, *Newfoundland,* the New Zealand *Achilles,* and the Canadian *Uganda* were given some operational training and experience in an air strike and bombardment on the Japanese base at Truk in the Carolines on June 14. By the end of the month the B.P.F. had re-assembled at Manus. When they sailed for the operational area on July 6, however, the *Indefatigable* had to be left behind owing to a breakdown of all her air compressors. Thus it was a force of only three carriers,

with one battleship, five cruisers, and 18 destroyers which on July 16, 1945 made rendezvous with the American force, now designated the 3rd Fleet, under Admiral William F. Halsey. This called for a change of the B.P.F.'s Task Force number to 37. A change in the command structure was to take place also. How it came about, the American C.-in-C. reveals in his autobiographical *Admiral Halsey's Story:*

"When I was informed at Pearl Harbor that the British Pacific Fleet would report to me, I naturally assumed that I would have full operational control, but when I re-read the plan at Leyte, I discovered that tactical control had been reserved. This would force me to present Admiral Rawlings with three alternatives and I did so now.

1. Task Force 37 would operate close aboard us as another Task Group in Task Force 38: it would not receive direct orders from me, but it would be privy to the orders I gave Task Force 38. These it would consider as suggestions to be followed to our mutual advantage, thereby assuring us a concentrated force with concentrated weapons.

2. Task Force 37 would operate semi-independently some 60 to 70 miles away, thereby preserving its technical identity at the cost of a divided force. (I stipulated that I would consent to this choice only if the request were put in writing.)

3. Task Force 37 would operate completely independently against soft spots in Japan which we would recommend if so desired.

Rawlings did not hesitate. He said, 'Of course, I'll accept No. 1'. My admiration for him began at that moment."

So, though the arrangement went far beyond what had been agreed at the highest levels, the B.P.F. was virtually absorbed into the U.S. 5th Fleet. No doubt it was inspired by Admiral Spruance's statement at the end of T.F.57's period under his overall command, that "the B.P.F. had gained sufficient experience to form part of the United States First Carrier Force". This was a real compliment to a force which had had to absorb in three months the expertise of carrier warfare over the vastness of the Pacific which the Americans had had more than three years to perfect. The B.P.F. accepted the situation with enthusiasm and strove to operate with

△ *Burial at sea.*

the same slick efficiency as their allies in spite of the very real handicaps of slower ships, of a multiplicity of aircraft types, of the need to fly aircraft on and off at shorter intervals owing to the low endurance of the Seafires, and the slower, less well-equipped tankers which made every refuelling an occasion for contrivance and improvisation followed by a high-speed dash through the night to rejoin the American part of the fleet.

The massed air attacks by the Japanese had petered out by the end of June. Now, until the end of the campaign, though there was still need for a defensive C.A.P. overhead (48 enemy aircraft were shot down over the fleet during July and August), the majority of the B.P.F.'s aircraft joined in the steady pounding of Japanese ports, shipping, and facilities which was intended as preparation for the final invasion. Surviving units of the Japanese fleet were sought out and made the object of special attention until all had been destroyed. On the night of July 18, the *King George V* and two Common-

wealth cruisers joined with American heavy units to hurl some 2,000 tons of shell into a factory area near Tokyo. On July 20 the *Indefatigable* rejoined, having completed repairs.

Meanwhile large reinforcements for the B.P.F. were gathering in Australian waters. They included the battleships *Duke of York* and *Anson,* the new light fleet carriers *Venerable, Colossus,* and *Vengeance,* and a number of cruisers and destroyers. They were too late to take an active part in the Pacific War.

On August 6 and 9, respectively, Hiroshima and Nagasaki were destroyed by atomic bombs; but it was not until the 14th that the Japanese capitulation was confirmed and operations ceased. From Task Force 37 a Task Group consisting of the *Indefatigable,* the battleship *Duke of York,* two cruisers, and ten destroyers was formed to remain with the 5th Fleet and be present at the formal Japanese surrender in Tokyo Bay. The remainder returned to Sydney – a first stop on the return journey to England.

▽ *Hellcat fighters line up for take-off.*

CHAPTER 166
Kamikaze: 'the divine wind'

by Jonathan Martin

On October 25, 1944, the Battle of Leyte Gulf was at its height. Shortly before 1100, the surviving ships of Rear-Admiral Clifford Sprague's "Taffy 3" escort carrier group were repairing damage caused during their engagement with Admiral Kurita's battleships and preparing to recover their aircraft. Inevitably the Americans were slightly off their guard when six "Zeke" (Mitsubishi A6M Zero) fighters swept in low over the sea towards them. Anti-aircraft guns engaged the attackers but, instead of attempting a conventional bombing or strafing attack, one of the Zekes roared over the stern of the St Lo and deliberately crash-dived onto the flight-deck amidships. The aircraft bounced overboard, but its bomb went through the deck and exploded.

Two minutes later a second explosion rocked the ship as the aviation fuel in the hangar went up. By 1100 hours the St Lo was aflame, and at 1121 she sank.

The other carriers were similarly attacked: Kalinin Bay was hit twice while a third aircraft crashed nearby; another missed the bridge of the Kitkun Bay but struck the port catwalk; and the sixth Zeke crashed astern of White Plains but caused only minor damage.

About 100 miles to the north another part of the escort force had a similar experience: at about 0740 hours four Zekes approached Rear-Admiral Thomas Sprague's "Taffy 1" at high altitude and dived on the carriers. The Santee was hit forward of the elevator while Sangamon and Petrof Bay suffered near misses. A

△ "The 89th Suicide Unit takes off from the Nakaminato base" by the Japanese artist Usaburo Ihara. The aircraft appear to be Nakajima Ki-43 Hayabusa single-seat fighters adapted to the rôle.

few minutes later the last aircraft hit the *Suwanee,* causing heavy casualties. However, all damage was repaired within two hours and the carriers were able to resume operating their aircraft.

The U.S. Pacific Fleet had suffered its first casualties from the *Kamikaze Tokubetsu Kogetikai* – the "Divine Wind Special Attack Force" of suicide pilots whose massive and despairing attacks were to horrify the Allied forces during the remainder of the war. Although October 25 saw the first mass suicide attacks, it was probably not the first action by the *kamikazes,* for on October 21, while supporting the Leyte landings, the cruiser *Australia* had been struck by a lone Zeke. This hit the bridge, killing 20 men (including the captain), wounding 54, and forcing the ship to retire from the battle zone.

These first suicide attacks and their evolution into the main offensive weapon of the Japanese during the last part of the war were born of despair. In June 1944 the last hopes that the Japanese Navy might have had of continuing to fight the Americans by conventional means had been shattered during the Battle of the Philippine Sea. In one day three carriers and more than 400 carrier-borne aircraft with 445 crew had been lost, while more than 100 land-based aircraft were also destroyed. The *matériel* cost was frightening, but what was even more serious was that these were the last even partially trained aircrews available. Now the bulk of the Japanese pilots were under-trained, outnumbered, and under-equipped, hitting only ten per cent of practice targets.

Faced with the fact that most of their men were going to almost certain and useless death, it was inevitable that naval officers should look desperately for more certain ways of attacking the enemy – and that the most dedicated of them should begin to think of the possibility of deliberately piloting their bombs into the enemy ships. During the summer of 1944, this idea was put forward by Rear-Admiral Sueo Obayashi, commander of the 3rd Carrier Division, and Captain Eichiro Iyo, commander of the carrier *Chiyoda,* to Admiral Ozawa, commander-in-chief of the carrier forces. Considerable impetus was given to their arguments by the action of the commander of the 26th Air Flotilla, Rear-Admiral Arima, who led a force against the American fleet off Luzon and appeared to crash his aircraft deliberately on the carrier *Franklin.*

The final impetus for setting up the first *kamikaze* units was provided by the inevitability of the American attack on the Philippine islands and the pitifully small Japanese force available to defend them. The Japanese were determined to hold the Philippines at all costs, since their loss would cut the home islands off from the essential oil and other supplies

of South-East Asia. The high command drew up Operation "SHO" (see Chapter 159).

Crucial to this plan was the neutralisation of American carrier-borne airpower, since if this were not done the battleships would be attacked and sunk long before they reached their goal. The main responsibility for this rested on the 1st Air Fleet in the Philippines. But the

△ △ *Four* kamikaze *pilots receive their final instructions.*
△ *Group photograph of some of Japan's élite* kamikaze *pilots. Note the parachute harnesses – which would be unnecessary on the pilots' only combat flight.*

1st Air Fleet simply did not have sufficient aircraft to have any chance of carrying out its task successfully. On September 9, the American fast carriers had blasted the main Japanese base on Davao, causing considerable damage. The main fighter force, which had been training at Clark Field on Luzon island, was immediately transferred to Cebu island to defend

Davao, but the Americans appeared to have withdrawn. However, two days later the Americans launched a surprise attack on Cebu, catching more than 100 Zekes lined up on the runway. Over 50 were destroyed and many others damaged; over two-thirds of the Japanese strength had been put out of action.

Reserves were called in urgently, but when, on October 17, Vice-Admiral Kaki-

jiro Ohnishi arrived to take over the 1st Air Fleet, only 30 Zekes and 30 bombers were operational. On the day of his arrival Ohnishi received instructions that Operation "SHO" had begun and that he should activate the aerial side of it.

Ohnishi was one of Japan's most experienced pilots, and had fought extensively in China. He had helped to plan the Pearl Harbor operation and had been one of Admiral Yamamoto's chief aides in the build-up of the Imperial Navy's air arm. A forceful, arrogant, but highly capable officer, he had no illusions about the impossibility of his task.

On October 19, Ohnishi went to the headquarters of Admiral Soemu Toyoda, Commander-in-Chief of the Combined Fleet, and put it to him that the only way to ensure that the American carriers were neutralised was by undertaking suicide attacks. Despite initial objections, Ohnishi received permission to set up the first attack groups, and during that afternoon he went to Mabalacat airfield where the 201st Air Group, with all the available Zeke fighters, was based. There he explained his ideas to the executive officer of the base, Asaicki Tamai, and the senior staff officer of the 1st Air Fleet, Rikihei Inoguchi.

Both were initially disconcerted by his suggestion that they should set up the first Special Attack Unit, but after discussion with the flight commanders, Tamai agreed to do so without delay. A 23-year-old regular officer, Lieutenant Yukio Seki, was selected as commander of the force, which was given the title "Shimpu" Attack Corps (another way of reading the characters for "kamikaze" –the name of the divine wind which had scattered the fleet of Genghis Khan during his attempted invasion of Japan in the 13th century). The first 24 volunteers were divided into four sections—Shikishima, Yamato, Asahi, and Yamazakura—named after the words of a patriotic poem.

The next day Commander Nakajima, adjutant of the 201st Air Group, flew to Cebu and there organised the setting up of a second unit. As at Mabalacat there was no difficulty in recruiting volunteers.

In fact, throughout its existence, the kamikaze corps—and the other methods of suicide attack which were developed—never lacked volunteers, although these might vary in their standards. Extreme patriotism, and acceptance by both military and civilians that they should serve Emperor and country even to the extent of deliberately laying down their lives, were a fundamental part of the traditions of pre-war Japan.

With several earlier examples, and the whole weight of national tradition behind them, it was not surprising that the Japanese leaders should have turned to mass suicide as a weapon of war, or that they should have found so many volunteers ready and eager to follow them.

The first flights of the *Shimpu* Attack Corps took place on October 21. Sixteen took off to attack the American carrier force supporting the Leyte landings, but inadequate reconnaissance meant that they were unable to locate the enemy and

well as Zekes. The 2nd Air Fleet, which had arrived in the Philippines on October 23 and undertaken several unsuccessful conventional attacks, was amalgamated with the 1st on October 26 and began preparing Special Attack Groups. The Army Air Force also prepared to follow the Navy's example.

Throughout the next three months, while the Americans struggled to reconquer the Philippines, they were subjected to unrelenting *kamikaze* attacks. One of the worst during the Leyte operations came on November 25 when six Zekes and two "Judies" (Yokosuka D4Y *Suisei* carrier bombers) attacked the fast

all but one aircraft returned to base. That aircraft may well have been the one which crashed onto *Australia*.

For the next three days, similarly unsuccessful flights were undertaken, but on October 25 came the attacks on "Taffy 1" and "Taffy 3", which resulted in the sinking of the *St Lo*. These two actions, in which ten aircraft were able to sink one carrier and damage five others, were seen as a triumphant vindication of the *kamikaze* idea. Admiral Ohnishi returned to Japan to request as many aircraft as possible for suicide attacks, while further units were set up, using a wide variety of aircraft, bombers and dive-bombers as

carrier task force. The fleet carrier *Essex*, two of her sister ships, and the light carrier *Independence* were hit. On December 13 more than 100 Japanese aircraft, about one-third of them *kamikazes*, attacked the U.S. forces gathering for the landing on Mindoro. The cruiser *Nashville*, flagship of the force, was hit and her flag bridge, combat information centre, and communications office were wrecked. Thereafter the U.S. ships were attacked almost every day until Japanese attention was switched to the ships preparing for the final landing at Lingayen Gulf.

On January 3, 1945 the escort carrier *Ommaney Bay* was so seriously damaged that she had to be abandoned and sunk. The luckless *Australia* was hit five times between January 6 and 9; although 44 men were killed and 72 wounded she was able to remain in action. During the landing the battleships *New Mexico* and *Colorado*, cruisers *Columbia* and *Louisville*, and 21 other vessels were hit.

To maintain this level of attack the Japanese set up a training base on Formosa where crews received a seven-day course in *kamikaze* tactics before being flown to the Philippines. Attack methods had been standardised using two main approaches: either at high altitude to about five miles from the target

October 25, 1944 and January 25, 1945, about 447 attacks were launched. Of these, 201 had been completed, 67 aircraft had been shot down by U.S. fighters or anti-aircraft fire, and 179 aircraft had returned to base after failing to locate targets. The American forces had lost two escort carriers and three destroyers, while 23 cruisers, five battleships, nine cruisers, 23 destroyers, and 27 other vessels had been damaged. The *kamikazes* had killed 738 men and wounded 1,300.

The airborne *kamikazes* had launched the most spectacular and numerous attacks of the campaign, but they had not been the only suicide units in action, for

followed by an ever-steepening dive, or a low level approach at about 30 feet above the sea followed by a climb to about 1,000 feet close to the target and a near-vertical dive. But the continual fighting and the nature of the weapon that they were using inevitably took its toll of Japanese strength. Early in January, the 1st Air Fleet flew its last mission with five Zekes and was then withdrawn to Formosa. The last major attacks of the campaign were launched on January 13, damaging the escort carrier *Salamaua* and the destroyer *Bagley,* and the last flight of all took place on January 25.

During the three months between

the Japanese Navy had been developing two other weapons which first went into action in the Philippines.

The first use of "human torpedoes" by the Japanese navy had been during the Russo-Japanese war; during the attack on Pearl Harbor two-man midget submarines had been deployed in an attempt to penetrate the anchorage. These had pointed the way for a development of the 24-inch Type 93 torpedo, the giant "Long Lance" which had created havoc amongst Allied surface units during the early engagements of the war. During the winter of 1942–3 two naval lieutenants and a naval architect, Hiroshi Suzukawa, developed a

△ ◁ *A Zero fighter on a* kamikaze *mission roars in towards the "Casablanca" class escort-carrier* White Plains.
△ *A* kamikaze *comes down over the "Cleveland/Fargo" class light cruiser* Vicksburg, *ex-*Cheyenne.

design for a piloted version of the Long Lance—which became known as the *Kaiten* ("Heaven Shaker"). This had an extra section, fitted aft of the warhead, which contained a compartment for the pilot and his controls. The size of the warhead was tripled to 3,400 lbs—reckoned to be enough to sink even the largest ships—and the range to an estimated 48 miles.

Plans were sent to the Naval General Staff during 1943 but no action was taken until after the disaster at the Battle of the Philippine Sea. Then a prototype was approved—although it was insisted that

some means of escape must be provided for the pilot—volunteers were called for, and a unit set up near Kure.

The first *Kaiten* strike was made in November against the American naval base at Ulithi by three fleet submarines each carrying four *Kaiten*. The force sailed on the 8th, but *I-37* was sunk by the U.S. destroyer *Nicholas* on November 12. On the 20th, *I-47* launched her four *Kaiten* off the coast of Ulithi. Three explosions were heard before the submarine set sail for home. U.S. destroyers attacked *I-36* when she had launched only one

Kaiten but she managed to escape and return to port. On the basis of the reported explosions and subsequent reconnaissance flights it was estimated that an aircraft carrier and two battleships had been sunk, and the operation was judged a great success. In reality, only the tanker *Mississinewa* had been sunk.

Plans were now drawn up for a more ambitious attack early in 1945 and during the first week of the year six submarines set sail with 24 *Kaiten* to strike at various U.S. anchorages. Between January 11 and 13, a total of 20 *Kaiten* was launched

against targets off New Guinea, the Palaus, the Admiralty Islands, and Guam. One exploded soon after leaving its mother ship, but the other 19 were again extravagantly credited with making 15 hits. None of these can be authenticated from American records, but the Japanese now envisaged a major increase in *Kaiten* activities. A new training centre was set up and 200 recruits began to learn the difficult art of controlling the *Kaiten*.

Several attempts were made to halt the Iwo Jima landings with *Kaiten*, but on no occasion were any launched since

the U.S. anti-submarine screen prevented the fleet submarines from getting close enough to their targets. The final attempt to operate the suicide torpedo was made on March 26 when four submarines with 18 *Kaiten* sailed to attack shipping off Okinawa. It was a complete failure, with two of the mother submarines being sunk before they reached the target area and the others so heavily attacked that they were barely able to escape without launching their weapons.

The other naval suicide weapon which was developed was the *Shinyo* suicide boat. This was about 18 feet in length and powered by one or two automobile engines. A high-explosive impact-fused warhead was carried in the bow and the maximum speed was between 25 and 30 knots. The type was used in the Philippine and Okinawa campaigns, and caused the loss of at least two destroyers, *Charles J. Badger* and *Hutchins.*

duced with the help of the Aeronautical Section of Tokyo University, created considerable interest amongst his superiors and in August an emergency development programme was set up at the Naval Air Research and Development centre. This, the *Marudai* project, resulted in the "*Okha*" ("Cherry Blossom") suicide bomb. Carried beneath a "Betty" (Mitsubishi G4M) bomber to within 20 miles of its target, the *Okha* 11 had a 2,646-lb warhead and was powered by three solid-propellant rockets which gave it a speed of about 400 mph.

In October Captain Motoharu Okamura was instructed to start recruiting and training pilots for *Jinrai Butai*, the "Corps of Divine Thunder", which would operate the new weapon. Early in November the *Okha* made its first successful flight and the first 50 to be completed were loaded on the new 68,000-ton carrier *Shinano* to be taken to Formosa. The

Once the Philippines had been secured, U.S. attacks moved to the very coasts of Japan. On February 10, 1945 Task Force 58, the U.S. fast carriers, sailed to strike at Tokyo and the air bases near it as a preparation for the attack on Iwo Jima. On February 19 the landings took place against fierce opposition but by March 17 the island had been completely occupied. There was virtually no *kamikaze* activity during the operation except for an attack on February 21 by aircraft from the 3rd Air Fleet in the Tokyo area which sank the escort carrier *Bismarck Sea* and damaged the *Saratoga,* forcing her to withdraw from the battle area.

During the summer of 1944 a junior pilot, Ensign Mitsuo Ota, had also come to the conclusion that the only way to make sure of hitting the enemy was to pilot the bomb right onto its target, and he had begun to draw up proposals for a special weapon. His first design, pro-

giant ship set sail from Yokosuka at the end of the month but on the 29th she was torpedoed four times by the U.S. submarine *Archerfish* and sank within two hours. No more *Okha* were yet available.

The next U.S. target was Okinawa, the first of the Japanese home islands to come within range. On land the commanding general made elaborate preparations for a defence to the last man, while the Japanese Navy drew up plans for massive suicide attacks against the American fleet. At the beginning of March the Japanese had just over 2,000 aircraft available for the defence of Okinawa. These were divided amongst four air fleets: 300 with the 1st on Formosa, 800 with the 3rd around Tokyo, 600 with the 5th on Kyūshū, and 400 with the 10th on Honshū.

Before the Americans launched their assault an attempt was made by the Japanese at a pre-emptive strike against

naissance report suggested that there was only one carrier at Ulithi. This was found to be false – there were, in fact, eight fleet carriers and seven escort carriers in the anchorage, but it was too late to continue the operation that day.

Early the next morning the aircraft took off again. The weather was bad and the *kamikazes* lost their guides. Thirteen of them developed engine trouble and had to return but the remaining 11 were able to reach the base unobserved and dive on the ships. Results were disappointing, for only one hit was made, causing damage to the carrier *Randolph*.

Between March 18 and 20 the invasion of Okinawa was heralded by a series of massive attacks made by Task Force 58 on targets on Kyūshū. About 50 *kamikazes* struck back, and the carrier *Franklin* was crippled, while hits were made on the *Essex, Wasp,* and *Enterprise*.

On the 21st a Japanese reconnaissance

the Pacific fleet's base at Ulithi. The attack was made by 24 "Frances" (Yokosuka P1Y *Ginga*) bombers, each carrying a 2,000-lb bomb and flown by a *kamikaze* pilot. The unit took off on March 10 guided by four flying boats, but before the aircraft were halfway to their objective they were recalled, since a recon-

▽ *The camera gun in an American fighter catches the destruction of a "Betty" bomber carrying an "Okha" (Cherry Blossom) suicide craft. The Americans dubbed this latter the "Baka" (Fool). The shifting horizon in the photographs is the result of the fighter jockeying for the best firing position.*

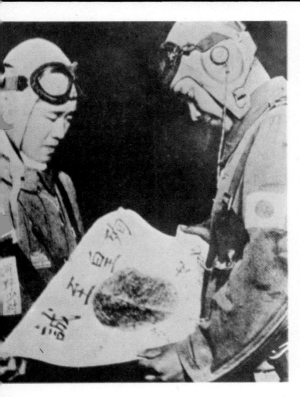

flight sighted three carriers apparently undefended and stationary about 350 miles off the coast. Vice-Admiral Ugaki, commander of the 5th Air Fleet, decided that this would be the ideal opportunity to try out the *Okha*. Eighteen were loaded onto their bombers and every available fighter was gathered to protect them. The Betty bomber was already totally outclassed, and when carrying the heavy *Okha* it was almost unmanoeuvrable. When it was found that only 55 Zekes were available, Commander Okamura's staff recommended that the operation should be abandoned since they reckoned that it would be impossible for the aircraft to get near enough to their targets before being shot down. But Ugaki, who had come to see the force take off, was insistent that they should go.

Eight Zekes were unable to take off because of mechanical faults and 17 of the remainder had to turn back. When the

△ ◁ *A kamikaze pilot adjusts a comrade's helmet and scarf just prior to a mission.*
◁ *Kamikaze pilots with ceremonial insignia.*

force was only 50 miles from the carriers' it was met by 50 Hellcats, which burst through the fighter screen and fell on the bombers. One was shot down immediately and although the remainder jettisoned their *Okhas* to take evasive action, 13 more were shot down in quick succession. The last four disappeared into clouds, hotly pursued by the Americans fighters, and were never seen again.

Thus ended the ignominious first sortie of the *Okha*. The only successful occasion on which they were used was on April 12, when eight bombers took off. Only two hits were made; one sinking the picket

were learning from experience and picket destroyers had been stationed around the island to give advance warning of the approach of *kamikazes*. They more than proved their worth, but these lightly armed ships turned out to have the most exposed task of any naval unit. Distributed singly or in pairs, and lacking fighter cover and massed gunfire support from other ships, they were an easy target and suffered very heavy casualties. Frequently the picket on a particular station had to be changed more than once a day because of battle damage, while one pair of destroyers reported more than 50

◁ *An* Okha *bomb, captured intact in its revetted hangar by American occupation forces when they arrived in Japan in 1945. The Japanese had had high hopes that the wide use of such weapons would inflict unacceptable losses on the Allies when they finally launched their invasion of the Japanese home islands.*

▷ *An* Okha *piloted bomb, taken on Okinawa, under examination at the Naval Aircraft Modification Unit at Johnsville, Pennsylvania. In the centre photograph a naval officer investigates the cockpit, and in the bottom one Lieutenant Wilson Pritchett takes a look at the three rocket motors.*

destroyer *Mannert L. Abele* and the other damaging the destroyer *Stanly*. In all some 800 *Okha* 11's were built, but only 74 were ever dispatched on missions and of these 56 were either jettisoned or shot down with their mother planes. Only four ever hit their targets.

While these attempts were being made to use the *Okha,* the *kamikazes* were engaged in their biggest and most savage battle. During the preliminary bombardment for the landing on Okinawa the cruiser *Indianapolis,* flagship of Admiral Spruance, the force commander, was put out of action. But the Americans

kamikaze attacks in less than 24 hours.

The Japanese defensive plan, codenamed "Kikusui" ("Floating Chrysanthemum", the crest of a 14th-century general who had led his army to certain death in a suicide operation), envisaged massive and co-ordinated *kamikaze* attacks on the landing forces, and the first of these was launched on April 6. Some 355 *kamikazes* swept at the American fleet, sinking two picket destroyers, two ammunition ships, and one L.S.T., and damaging more than 22 others.

On the same day the other part of the *Kikusui* operation began – the final

suicide charge of the remnants of the Japanese fleet. The super-battleship *Yamato*, the cruiser *Yahagi*, and eight destroyers set sail for Okinawa with only sufficient fuel to enable them to reach the island. Once there they would beach themselves in front of the U.S. fleet and fight until their ammunition was exhausted or they were totally destroyed. Sighted by U.S. submarines, they were heavily attacked by aircraft on the 7th and the *Yamato, Yahagi,* and four destroyers were sunk.

On the 11th the *kamikazes* made an attempt to get through to the carriers of Task Force 58, which was stationed off the north of Okinawa to provide air cover and act as a diversionary target for suicide pilots. Attacks were launched throughout the day, but no direct hits were made. Eight near misses caused minor damage to the battleship *Missouri* and the carrier *Enterprise*. The next day, the attacks were switched back to the pickets and landing support ships. Some 185 *kamikaze* attacks were launched, of which 151 were shot down before they reached their targets. The remainder succeeded in sinking a destroyer and damaging three battleships and six destroyers or escort destroyers.

Almost every day off Okinawa the American naval forces were subjected to some *kamikaze* attacks. But the main Japanese assaults against the ships lying off the beach-head came in ten major attacks–the third of which took place on August 16 with 165 aircraft, but little major damage ensued.

By the beginning of May, the savage rate of the earlier fighting was inevitably taking its toll on the Japanese. The numbers of aircraft and trained crews had fallen off drastically and the American defences were steadily improving. In the last major attack, on May 11, 72 *kamikazes* were shot down before they reached their targets. Two managed to hit Task Force 58's flagship, *Bunker Hill*, forcing Vice-Admiral Mitscher to transfer to *Enterprise*. The next day, he detached two task groups to raid Kyūshū. Considerable damage was caused, but during the operation *Enterprise* was hit by a *kamikaze* and Mitscher was forced to transfer his flag yet again, this time to the *Randolph*.

The last attacks by the *kamikazes* during the Okinawa campaign came on June 21 and 22, but little damage was caused. On July 2 the island was finally secure–the Americans having lost 26

The Japanese Mitsubishi G4M2e Model 24J ''Betty'' transport and Yokosuka MXY7 Model 11 ''Okha'' (Cherry blossom) suicide aircraft

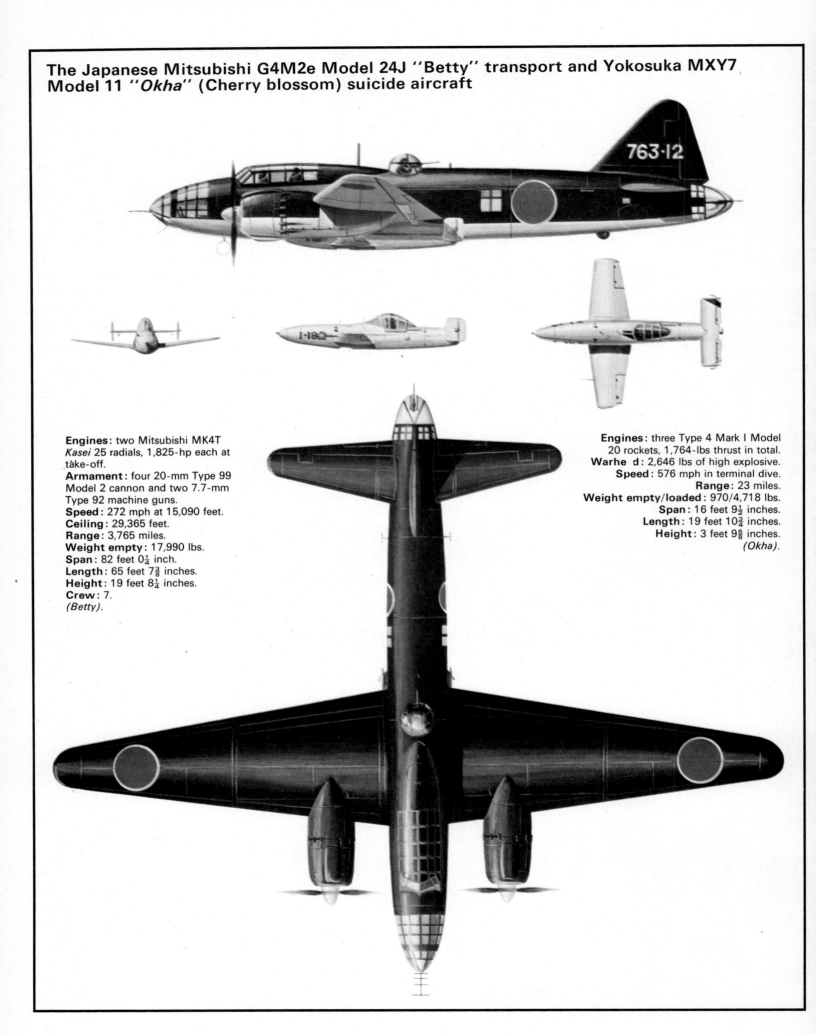

Engines: two Mitsubishi MK4T *Kasei* 25 radials, 1,825-hp each at take-off.
Armament: four 20-mm Type 99 Model 2 cannon and two 7.7-mm Type 92 machine guns.
Speed: 272 mph at 15,090 feet.
Ceiling: 29,365 feet.
Range: 3,765 miles.
Weight empty: 17,990 lbs.
Span: 82 feet 0¼ inch.
Length: 65 feet 7⅜ inches.
Height: 19 feet 8¼ inches.
Crew: 7.
(Betty).

Engines: three Type 4 Mark I Model 20 rockets, 1,764-lbs thrust in total.
Warhe d: 2,646 lbs of high explosive.
Speed: 576 mph in terminal dive.
Range: 23 miles.
Weight empty/loaded: 970/4,718 lbs.
Span: 16 feet 9½ inches.
Length: 19 feet 10¾ inches.
Height: 3 feet 9⅝ inches.
(Okha).

△ An American officer "takes a spin" in one of the 300 "Shinyo" suicide craft captured by the U.S. forces in the Kerama island group off the south-west coast of Okinawa. Launched from the beach by trolleys, the boats were painted dark green to blend with the background foliage. The two angled metal contraptions at the stern are launchers for 5-inch rockets, intended to put off the aim of the American light defences by shooting out a cloud of incendiary bullets. The boats displaced up to two tons, were $16\frac{1}{2}$ to 18 feet long and capable of speeds of between 25 and 30 knots, and were armed with a 4,406-lb warhead or two depth charges, fused to detonate on impact.

◁ A Japanese human torpedo on its launching rails.

△ ◁ *and* △ *Scenes on board a
British fleet carrier of Task
Group 57.2 (the 1st Aircraft-
Carrier Squadron) of Task Force
57, the British Carrier Force.*
◁ *Fire-fighting on board the
fleet carrier* Formidable, *hit by
a Zero at 1131 on May 4, 1945
during the Sakishima Gunto
operations. The armoured flight
deck proved its worth here,
although eight men were killed
and 47 wounded, with 11 aircraft
destroyed.*

ships to suicide attacks with a further 164 damaged. Approximately 1,465 *kamikaze* aircraft had taken part in the largest suicide operation of the war.

The Royal Navy had also been involved with the *kamikazes* during the Okinawa operation. Task Force 57 of four carriers and two battleships had joined the U.S. fleet on March 16 with the job of neutralising the Sakishima Gunto island group to the east of Formosa. It suffered frequent attacks, and hits were made on the carriers *Indefatigable, Formidable,* and *Victorious,* but it was found that the armoured decks of the British carriers gave them considerably better protection than the wooden decks of the American ships and none was out of action for more

ing up the American invasion force before it reached the shore fell on the *kamikazes.* Thousands of pilots were recruited and hastily trained for suicide attacks. Small emergency airstrips were built up and down the coasts. The *kamikazes* were to be dispersed on these so as to be relatively immune from enemy attack before flying off on their one-way missions. More than 5,300 aircraft of all types (ranging from fighters and bombers to training aircraft and flying boats) were available for suicide attacks; a further 5,000 would undertake escort duties and conventional attacks. Once all the *kamikazes* had been used these aircraft would take their place. Over 700 *Okha* 11's were available and the Japanese

▷ Kamikaze *pilots receive their ceremonial cup of* sake *before departing on their last flight.*
▷▷△ *During the American carrier sweep off Kyūshū: a "Judy" (Yokosuka D4Y* Suisei) *carrier-borne dive-bomber hurtles down towards the sea in flames after being hit by American A.A. fire. On suicide missions the type could carry a 1,764-lb bomb-load.*
▷▷▽ *A "Betty" hits the sea astern of an "Essex" class fleet carrier.*

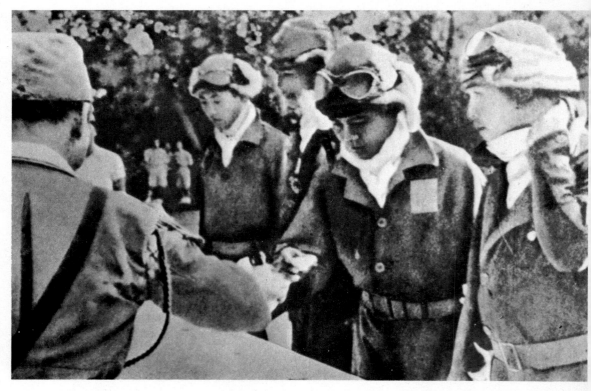

than a few hours.

It was now obvious that the next Allied objective must be an invasion of Japan. Despite its hopeless position, lacking a surface fleet, experienced pilots, or sufficient fuel to operate most weapons, and with its cities being devastated every day by the Superfortresses of the U.S. Air Force, the Japanese Government–largely forced by the intransigence of the army leaders–was determined to fight on. As the Allied planners worked on Operation "Olympic", the largest amphibious operation ever envisaged, which was to begin with a landing on Kyūshū on November 1, 1945, the Japanese prepared their defences.

Once again the responsibility for break-

were hurrying to produce other designs for rocket or ramjet powered variants.

Backing this aerial armada would be more than 400 *Koryu* and *Kairyu* suicide submarines (five- and two-man developments of the *Kaiten*) and at least 2,000 *Shinyo* suicide boats. Finally, and most bizarre of all, were the *Fukuyuru,* strong swimmers who would swim carrying mines on their backs to explode against Allied ships.

The stage was set for the greatest act of mass suicide in history when on August 6 an atomic bomb was dropped on Hiroshima. Three days later a second bomb on Nagasaki at last gave the Japanese leaders the face-saving excuse they needed to accept the inevitable and surrender.

On August 14 Naval Imperial Head-quarters ordered that all *kamikaze* operations should be suspended.

Many Japanese refused to accept what they saw as national disgrace. More than 1,000 army officers and many hundreds of naval officers and civilians took their own lives. Among them the originator of the first *kamikaze* operations, Admiral Ohnishi, who disembowelled himself in the traditional manner on August 16. Refusing the coup-de-grâce, he died in agony several hours later, leaving a message that he apologised with his death to the souls of the men he had ordered to their doom, and to their bereaved families.

One of his subordinates took a more spectacular way out. On hearing the order to suspend operations, Vice-Admiral Ugaki, determined to die in the same way as his men, ordered three aircraft to be prepared at Oita airfield. He took off on August 14, followed by ten other aircraft piloted by aircrew determined to follow his example, and headed for Okinawa. None of them returned, but it is symbolic of the ultimate futility of the *kamikazes* that no attacks were reported on any Allied ships during that day.

The *kamikazes* had cost the Allied forces more than lives and added immensely to the strain of operations in the Pacific theatre. But ultimately, as a weapon of despair, they were powerless to halt the steady build-up of American power and its advance to the coasts of Japan. Brought up with centuries of tradition of the sanctity of human life, the Western mind finds it difficult to comprehend how thousands of men could have volunteered deliberately to take their own lives. For this decision was not even made in the heat of battle. A *kamikaze* volunteer might have to wait weeks, or even months, before going into action, and during that time he had to live with the reality that every day might be his last. Yet there are no records of *kamikaze* pilots deliberately going back on their decision. Morale in all units was high and men actually competed to be allowed to go on operational missions. Only if one remembers and tries to understand the background within which these men were brought up and the massive weight of tradition which saw death in battle and suicide as noble and honourable institutions is it possible to understand something of the mentality which gave birth to and sustained the *kamikaze* operations.

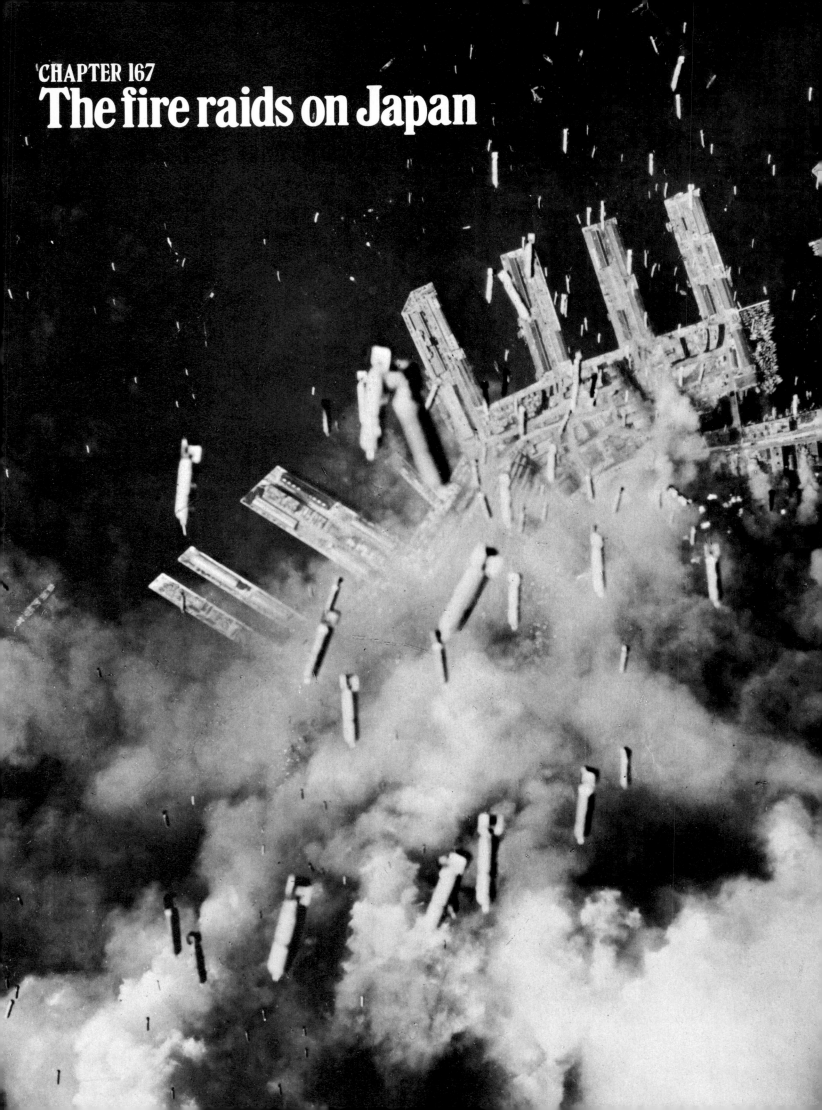

CHAPTER 167

The fire raids on Japan

As late as March 6, 1945 Major-General Curtis E. LeMay, who had recently replaced Brigadier-General H. S. Hansell as commander of the 21st Bomber Command, remarked: "This outfit has been getting a lot of publicity without having really accomplished a hell of a lot in bombing results."

To date, the tactics employed had been high level precision attacks by B-29's. However ice, high winds, poor visibility, and air turbulence made navigation and accurate bombing very difficult and it had taken up to eight separate H.E. raids to have any appreciable effect on some targets.

Late in 1944 the B-29's had been moved from China and India to bases on Saipan,

Guam, and Tinian in the Marianas. They made their first raid on Truk on October 28, and on November 24 they hit Tokyo.

Japanese fighter attacks from Iwo Jima were eliminated when the island was secured in March 1945, and its landing grounds subsequently saved the lives of 24,761 men in 2,251 emergency landings by crippled B-29's.

Since high altitude daylight raids were not giving good results, LeMay, who was by nature an experimenter, decided to test the effectiveness of incendiary bombs against these targets. The attack would be a massed assault against the industrial cities, delivered at low level, at night.

Two light test raids were made against Nagoya on January 3, and Kobe on

◁ *Bombs tumble down from U.S. Superfortress bombers onto the already blazing waterfront of a Japanese port.*
△ *A B-29 Superfortress unloads over Anshan in Manchuria, home of the Showa steel works. This was the second largest integrated iron and steel works in the Japanese system, and played a key part in Japan's development of her colony of Manchuria as an industrial entity.*

2791

February 4. The planners were pleased in the United States and a full-scale operation was suggested to evaluate the effectiveness of this type of attack. It was mounted on the nights of March 9–10, 1945, and the target was Tokyo.

LeMay staked his career on the operation, for many pessimists had predicted that at low level the B-29's would suffer very heavy losses. To increase the bombload, and prevent the aircraft from firing at one another in the dark, he had ordered that they should fly with unloaded guns. In place of the 8,000 rounds of machine gun ammunition normally carried, they added 3,200 pounds of bombs. In addition, the low-level approach would save the engines and further increase the bomb-load. On average each plane would carry six tons.

The lead squadron was loaded with 180 M47 70-pound napalm bombs which were to start fires to bring out the motorised fire-fighting equipment. The planes which followed would carry 24 500-pound clusters of M69's, a six-pound oil incendiary, very effective against lightly constructed buildings. These clusters were set to burst so that they would give a minimum density of 25 tons, or 8,333 M69's, per square mile.

The 334 B-29's, loaded with about 2,000 tons of bombs, came over the area in three wings at altitudes between 4,900 and 9,200 feet. The weather was better than usual with little cloud cover and a visibility of ten miles. As they unloaded their bombs, the crews saw the flames spread to form bigger fires.

The crews reported they could bomb visually and were meeting only light A.A. fire, with no fighter opposition. Later formations found the target obscured by smoke and had to range wide over the area in search of new targets. Turbulence from the fires made the bomb runs difficult as the aircraft rose in the intense heat waves. On the return flight, tail gunners could see a glow for 150 miles.

For the raiders it was an inexpensive attack; flak damaged 42 bombers, 14 were lost, and of these the crews of five were rescued. The loss ratio was 4.2 per cent, which compared well with the 3.5 per cent figure for all B-29 raids and the 5.7 for January.

For the inhabitants of Tokyo it was a horrifying and awesome experience. Police records show that 267,171 buildings were destroyed and 1,008,005 people made homeless. There were 83,793 dead and 40,918 wounded, and it was nearly a month before the last body was removed from the ruins.

Photographs revealed that 15.8 square miles of the city had been burnt out; this included 18 per cent of the industrial area and 63 per cent of the commercial centre and the heart of the congested residential area. The Intelligence officers of the 21st Bomber Command removed 21 numbered industrial plants from their target lists.

Less than 24 hours after this attack a force of 313 B-29's began taking off on the afternoon of March 11 with the target of Nagoya, Japan's third largest city and centre of her aircraft industry. One aircraft ditched on take off, and 19

◁ *American groundcrew load clusters of incendiary bombs into a medium bomber. The same type of incendiary was used to help burn out the heart of Japan.*
△ *Part of the horrific aftermath of a fire raid on Tokyo: the bodies of hundreds of burnt men, women, and children litter the streets of the capital after the all-clear.*

▽ *The remains of a components assembly hall in one of the Mitsubishi plants at Nagoya, after a B-29 raid from the Marianas. Mitsubishi was the largest aircraft engine, and second largest airframe, constructor in Japan.*

others turned back with mechanical trouble. The 285 which reached the city unloaded 1,790 tons of incendiary bombs from between 5,100 and 8,500 feet. Despite the fact that the bomb-load was 125 tons heavier than that dropped on Tokyo, there was no general holocaust.

There were 394 separate fires, and post-strike photographs revealed that 2.05 square miles of the city had been destroyed. Though 18 numbered industrial targets (that is plants given a special designation in target folders) were damaged or destroyed, the aircraft plants were not knocked out.

Nagoya survived because it had an adequate water supply, well-spaced fire breaks, an efficient fire-fighting service which operated promptly and effectively, and that night there was no wind to fan the initial fires into bigger blazes.

For the raiders the attack was again an inexpensive operation – the only bomber lost was the one that ditched at take off.

major road and rail links, it was a great commercial and administrative centre. In 1945 it had an estimated population of 2,142,480.

Like other major cities, it was congested and inflammable. It had never been hit before by any major strikes, and now stood ready for destruction by fire.

On March 13, after heroic efforts by the maintenance crews, 301 B-29's took off, each carrying six tons of bombs, and this time the low wing carried .50-inch ammunition for lower forward and aft turrets as well as for the tail guns. The target was obscured by clouds when the 274 bombers that reached Osaka began their run. Using radar they achieved a better concentration than the attack on Nagoya.

In three hours they dropped 1,732.6 tons of bombs and burned out 8.1 square miles of the city centre. As the flames increased, fire fighting and A.R.P. services collapsed, and 119 major factories

△ A Superfortress takes off from Harmon Field on Guam for a mission over Japan. The capture of the Marianas, of which Guam is one, had featured in U.S. plans particularly as air bases for the giant B-29 bombers could be built there.

Twenty others were damaged, 18 by flak and two by fighters.

Osaka was the next target. The city produced about one-tenth of Japan's war-time total of ships, one-seventh of her electrical equipment, and one-third of her machinery and machine tools. Its army arsenal furnished 20 per cent of the army's ordnance requirements, and though it did not assemble aircraft, Osaka contained many sub-contractors producing engine parts. Besides having

were destroyed and 134,744 houses burned down, with 1,363 damaged. The Osaka fire department listed 3,988 dead, 678 missing, and 8,463 injured. It was the Tokyo fire-storm again, with men and women suffocating in makeshift shelters or roasted alive as they rushed through the flames.

Now it was the turn of Japan's sixth largest city. On March 16 the bombers came to Kobe. Like Osaka it was "practically a virgin target".

A port with a long irregular water front, it was easy to pick out on a radar scope. On either side of the harbour were important heavy industrial installations. It was Japan's most important overseas port and a focus for inland transportation.

The bomb-load for the attack was different this time because the earlier operations had used up nearly all the available stocks of M47's and M69's. The B-29's would be carrying M17A1's, 500-pound clusters of 4-pound magnesium thermite incendiaries. While these bombs would be effective against the dockland and industrial buildings, they would have less impact on the flimsy houses.

In two hours and eight minutes, 307 bombers unloaded 2,355 tons. Japanese fighters were up this time, but they did not interfere with the raid–though they made 93 attacks, none of the three B-29's lost was hit by fighters.

The post-attack photographs looked disappointing. Only 2.9 square miles

The March campaign was brought to a close with a return visit to Nagoya on the night of the 19th. The bomb loads carried by the different wings reflected the way the fire raids had used up the available stocks of incendiaries. Every third plane carried two 500-pound general purpose H.E. bombs to disorganise the fire-fighters. The 314th Wing carried M69's, the 313th M47's, and the 73rd a mixed load of M47's and M76's.

A total of 1,858 tons of bombs was dropped by the 290 aircraft which reached Nagoya, and because of smoke and search-lights, the bomb aimers had to use radar. This time they burned out three square miles and damaged the Nagoya arsenal, the marshalling yards, and the Aichi engine factory; but the Mitsubishi plants escaped with minor damage.

It had been a good month for the 21st Bomber Command. It had flown 1,595 sorties in 10 days (three-fourths as many as had been flown in all previous missions)

(about a fifth of the city) had been destroyed. However, on the ground the Japanese could assess the cost in human and industrial losses more accurately. About 500 industrial buildings were destroyed and 162 damaged. Among those heavily damaged were the Kawasaki shipyards, where 2,000-ton submarines were built. The loss of 65,951 houses left 242,468 people homeless. Police records showed 2,669 dead or missing and 11,289 injured.

and the 9,365 tons of bombs dropped were three times the weight expended before March 9.

Though there had been a great strain on both flight and maintenance crews, they had recovered quickly and morale was very high. Men and machines had shown that they could achieve spectacular results for a loss ratio of 0.9 per cent in crew, far lower than that for day-light missions. The lower altitudes allowed a higher bomb-load to be carried and caused less wear on the engines. In Washington and Guam the planners adjusted their target programme and prepared a three-phase list with 33 targets rated A, B, or C according to their relative industrial value. Some like Nagoya, Osaka, and Kobe had been hit before, but the planners felt that some of their urban areas still merited attention. The first phase emphasised the destruction of ground ordnance and aircraft plants, the second machine tools, electrical equipment, and ordnance and aircraft parts. Phase three would be implemented in the light of the results from the first 22 targets.

And what of Japan? The attacks had left behind 32 square miles of cinders and fire-blackened buildings in four major cities. Not only had strategic targets been destroyed, but factories producing goods for home consumption. Workers lost their homes, or accommodation in factory dormitories, and the evacuation which followed added to the labour problems already caused by the conscription of adult males. Early in 1944 some 600,000 houses were demolished to provide fire breaks, and since building materials were not provided, the destitute families had to find shelter with friends and relatives, or in public buildings. Natural disasters added to their misery, for 1945 was a year of excessive rainfall and floods. Local fires and earthquakes destroyed a further 500,000 houses. By July about a quarter of all the houses in Japan had been destroyed by all causes and some 22 million people, about three-tenths of the population, had been made homeless.

Operations in support of the landings at Okinawa diverted the bombers from major incendiary attacks for two months. The savage fighting for the island, and the suicidal attacks on shipping, convinced LeMay that he should try to bomb Japan into surrender, rather than see this slaughter repeated on a larger scale in the invasion of the main islands.

The new campaign was inaugurated with a day-light attack on Nagoya on May 14. A total of 472 bombers dropped 2,515 tons of M69's from between 12,000 and 20,500 feet. Though the raid burned only about 3.15 square miles, Mitsubishi's No. 10 engine works lost its Kelmut bearing plant and suffered other damage.

An attack on the docks and industrial areas to the south on the night of May 16 showed how effective low-level night attacks were in contrast to the day-light high-level operations. In the May

14 raid ten B-29's were lost, two to enemy action. The night attack had only three losses, all due to mechanical failure. As it was a low-level attack, the aircraft carried eight tons as against 5.3 on day-light raids, and so a total of 3,609 tons of mixed M47's and M50's were dropped. The raid burned 3.82 square miles and heavily damaged Mitsubishi's No. 5 aircraft works. Nagoya was finished as a target for area attacks.

Little purpose is served in detailing all the raids made between May and June. With variations such as day-light escorted operations, or mixed bomb-loads, they brought fiery destruction to the major cities of Japan.

	Total urban area	Destroyed
City	(in square miles)	
Tokyo	110.8	56.3
Nagoya	39.7	12.4
Kobe	15.7	8.8
Osaka	59.8	15.6
Yokohama	20.2	8.9
Kawasaki	11.0	3.6
Totals	257.2	105.6

△ *A box of B-29's wings its late afternoon way over the Pacific en route for a night mission over the Japanese homeland.*
△▷ *Bombs cascade from the bellies of American Superfortress bombers.*
▷ *A B-29 returning from a raid on Japan lands on the emergency strip built at Motoyama on Iwo Jima. U.S. Marines flock to examine the bomber and greet the crew.*

The Japanese capital received a double knock-out blow on the nights of May 23 and 25. In previous raids 5,000 tons of bombs had destroyed 34.2 square miles, and 2,545 tons had been expended in precision attacks.

In the first raid, for the loss of 17 bombers, 520 B-29's dropped 3,646 tons of bombs and destroyed 5.3 square miles.

The second raid brought the bombers close to the Imperial Palace and "took out" parts of the financial, commercial, and governmental districts of the city. The bomb-load was lighter, but some 3,262 tons dropped by 502 aircraft yielded results which had not been anticipated: 16.8 square miles, the greatest area destroyed in a single raid, lay smoking beneath the reconnaissance aircraft when they visited the city.

With 50.8 per cent of the entire city reduced to ashes and rubble, Tokyo was removed from the list of incendiary targets.

In the campaign some 4,678 sorties were flown and 27,164 tons of bombs dropped. And for the loss of 70 aircraft and damage to 420, a further 48 square miles of target areas were burned out. But there still remained the smaller cities undamaged by fire, and now they experienced the terror by night.

Sixty attacks, following the same tactics employed against the main targets, were made between June 17 and August 14. As a rule a B-29 wing would take one city, and in this way four targets could be attacked on one night. The 21st Bomber Command flew 8,014 sorties and dropped 54,184 tons of incendiaries, and for the loss of 19 bombers destroyed 63.75 square miles, about half the total area of all the targets.

Such was their confidence, the Americans now dropped leaflets to warn the civilians in these cities before they struck. But while 12 cities would receive the leaflets, only four would be attacked. Despite this, the people poured into the country. Sensing the desperate mood of the nation, the Minister of Home Affairs, Motoki Abe, said later: "I believe that after the 23–24 May (sic) 1945 raids on Tokyo, civilian defence measures in that city, as well as other parts of Japan, were considered a futile effort." But Mamoru Shigemitsu, the Foreign Minister, asserted that though "day by day Japan turned into a furnace . . . the clarion call was accepted. If the Emperor ordained it, they would leap into the flames. That was the people of Japan."

△ ◁ ◁ *Crew of "Waddy's Wagon", the fifth B-29 to take off on the first Tokyo mission from Saipan and the first to land: Capt. "Waddy" Young (captain), Lt. Jack Vetters (pilot), Lt. John Ellis (bombardier), Lt. Paul Garrison (navigator), Sgt. George Avon (radio operator), Lt. Bernard Black (engineer), Sgt. Kenneth Mansio (engineer), and Sgts. Lawrence Lee, Wilbur Chapman, Corbett Carnegie, and Joe Gatto (gunners).*
△ ◁ *and* △ *Civilians leave Tokyo for the safety of the country.*
◁ *Superfortresses pass over the Marianas en route to Japan.*
▽ ◁ *Emperor Hirohito inspects some of the damage to Tokyo.*
▽ *Burnt-out Tokyo, with only the shells of concrete buildings left standing. In the foreground is the Hihonbashi area, and across the Sumida river the Koto ward.*

The American Boeing B-29 Superfortress heavy bomber

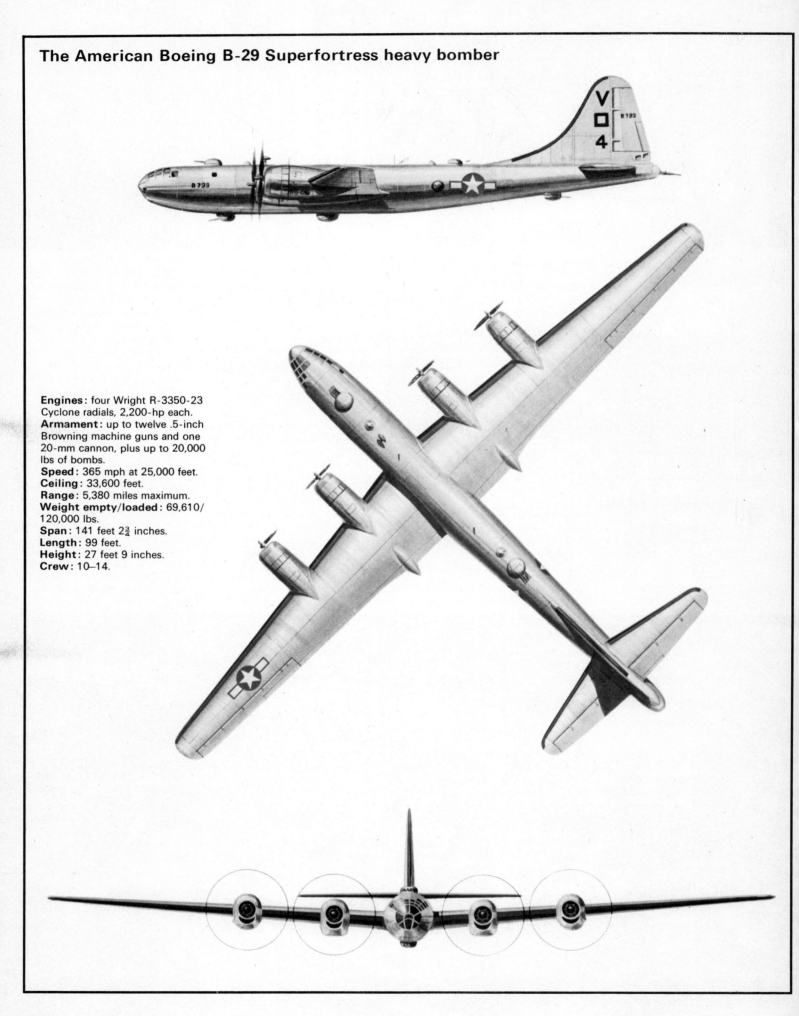

Engines: four Wright R-3350-23 Cyclone radials, 2,200-hp each.
Armament: up to twelve .5-inch Browning machine guns and one 20-mm cannon, plus up to 20,000 lbs of bombs.
Speed: 365 mph at 25,000 feet.
Ceiling: 33,600 feet.
Range: 5,380 miles maximum.
Weight empty/loaded: 69,610/120,000 lbs.
Span: 141 feet 2¾ inches.
Length: 99 feet.
Height: 27 feet 9 inches.
Crew: 10–14.